Judge [Ret.] Schafer's Professional Background

Trial Attorney, U.S. Department of Justice, Wash., D.C.
Assistant U.S. Attorney, Ketchikan, Alaska
Deputy Pima County Attorney, Tucson, Ariz.
Chief Deputy Pima County Attorney
Assistant Arizona Attorney General, Phoenix, Ariz.
Chief Counsel, Criminal Division, Arizona Attorney General
Arizona State Superior Court Judge, Phoenix, Ariz.

Cover Art by Cory After Spy

Phoenix, Arizona

©

Copyright 2014

TABLE OF CONTENTS

A Most Curious Murder Case [Page 53]
[True Story]
Simplicio Torrez stole a horse and killed the town Marshall of Williams, Arizona, as he was being arrested. He had a feeble insanity defense and was convicted and given a death sentence. His attorney filed an appeal – or did he?

Franco's Coat [Page 59]
[True story]
Occasionally after a burglary the victim will tell the police that something was stolen that was not. He's planning to collect insurance. I had a case like that years ago with a surprise ending.

A True and Accurate Account of the Execution of Eva Dugan
[True story] [Page 64]
Ms. Eva Dugan arrived in Tucson by train with no plans or money. She quickly hooked up with a farmer and a hired hand. Soon she ran off with the hand and stole the farmer's money and car. After she left, the farmer could not be found. She was sent to prison for stealing his car and later when they found his body she was tried for his murder, convicted and hanged. People do not remember much about the trial; it's the execution they remember.

The Most Dangerous Rat [Page 71]
[True story]
In 1934 John Dillinger was a nationally known thug whose bank robberies established a template for robbery and who became infamous for his good looks and daring. After a shootout in Wisconsin he and his gang decided to take a vacation in Tucson and that's where he was captured by a back-water dinky police department without firing a shot.

Rules of Court [Page 78]
[True]
Rules of Deportment for Division 218 of the Superior Court

The Inheritors

Gregory, quite understandably, had been on edge for days.

"Why do you suppose he has called us here?" he asked, nervously pacing the floor of my suite.

"Only heaven can hazard a guess, Gregory, but whatever it is, you can wager it is important."

I could not help but sense the humor in the situation. Sir Melvin, Lord of Farnsworth, had not seen his immediate family in years, excluding me of course; the proximity of my dwelling to his estate did shape a certain bond between us, and now he had summoned all of us to Farnsworth. Gregory, who was last in succession and only the Queen knows where in the Lord's estimation, had received his cable a day late and he strongly suspected that it was more than a mere oversight by the aged benefactor.

Gregory fumbled in his breast pocket and pulled out a long slender yellowish cigarette. He fumbled at lighting it and molten tobacco fell on his lapel.

"Oh, honestly," he sighed. "First the tennis mess and now this."

Gregory was a man of circumstances - all of them notoriously questionable. It was not that there was any maliciousness in his makeup; it was more as though he had irreparably bruised the funny bone of the gods at a very early age. And since that time, a sort of inverse Midas' touch had lurked about him, showing itself only at the most inopportune times.

There was that horribly abortive year at Sandhurst; the abrupt exile to Brussels when his passport was held for a month; that small affair with the housekeeper in Kent that ended in the tabloids, and that blighted summer at Whetson when he lost his auto in the bay. Then the growth of that square, rather rakish mustache that still adorned his face. It was approximately two years ago, I believe, when I first noticed a bit of something shadowing his upper lip. As I recall, he explained it as a sort of metabolic bandage for a rugby scar. The weekend edition of the Gazette, however, had a far different and simpler explanation involving a cigarette burn at Mrs. Lockwood's Rooms. And finally there was that difficult period of readjustment after his father's death. He had expected, of course, that whatever monies had been tied up in insurance and the estate would be divided among the heirs, but much to his consternation the entire estate was put back into the barrel factory and Gregory was left the management. And in four short years he had quietly mismanaged the company into a progressive state of bankruptcy.

As I glanced at his reflection in the mirror I smiled.

He caught my glance. "Oh, really, David, I've got a great deal at stake here. I've been courting this inheritance for quite some time. And frankly if..if..."

His voice broke and he sat down.

I glanced at my watch. "Jove, Gregory, we had better get a start on; they'll be carrying on without us."

A cab was summoned and we made our way to Farnsworth.

The first round of cocktails had barely disappeared when we arrived. Sir Melvin caught my eye and beckoned me to him. Sir Melvin was a short squatty man with a very large protruding stomach. His head was bald and his skin, which was splotched with red, slid down to his jowls.

"Ah, David, pleasure to see you," he said.

Gregory had positioned himself behind me. Sir Melvin rose on his toes and peered over my shoulder.

"And, Gregory," he said in a bland tone.

Gregory nodded.

"This, gentlemen," said Sir Melvin, turning to a younger man beside him, "is my solicitor, Mr. Christopher Smail."

I extended my hand to the younger gentleman. Gregory slid from behind my back, shook Mr. Smail's hand and then retreated slowly. Mr. Smail was a tall man with a thin mustache. He stood very straight and when he spoke he put his hand in and out of his coat pocket.

Sir Melvin stepped to the middle of the room. Sensing that the moment had arrived, the assembled heirs took their chairs and clustered - at a safe distance, of course - about him. As he studied the design in the carpet he said, "It must be evident that when I pass beyond, each of you stands to inherit a sizeable annuity."

There was a general relaxation about the room. Gregory sat back and crossed his legs.

"But there is," he continued, "a frightful thing to deal with - the inheritance tax. It's rather large. That is why I have summoned my solicitor, Mr. Smail, here tonight. He has devised a plan whereby each of you may avoid this tax. Now, it is a bit tricky, but I believe that if you will bear with us, you will see the wisdom in it. Christopher, please."

Mr. Smail cleared his throat and studied the heirs as though he was looking for someone he knew.

"I will try to make this as elementary as possible," he said. He scratched the side of his face and ran his index finger over his mustache.

"When Sir Melvin expires each of you will inherit one eighth of his estate, and a tax on that inheritance must be paid. Now, if Sir Melvin, instead of leaving you this money by will, were to make you a gift of it at the present time, there would be no tax, because Parliament does not exact a tax on gifts. Is that clear?"

He looked about the room and seeing no questions, continued. "Well, with this in mind then, I have suggested to Sir Melvin that he convert his holdings into cash immediately and give to each of you his due share now. However," and he paused, "there is one drawback to a gift."

A silence fell on the room. Gregory eased himself to the edge of his chair. Mr. Smail continued.

"This trick of avoiding the inheritance tax has been tried before and in many instances the giver has died within a few months of making the gift. Consequently, a few years ago Parliament decreed that a gift will not be valid unless the giver lives for one year thereafter. If the giver should die within that year the gift is automatically revoked and the money passes as if given by will - and in that event the inheritance tax must then be paid. Of course in our case, with so robust a man as Sir Melvin this is a mere technicality. In one year from tonight the money will be distributed free of inheritance tax."

Gregory sat quietly folded up in the rear of the cab running his fingers through the moisture on the window.

"Do you think the old boy can hold on for a year?"

"He ruddy-well better," I chuckled.

Gregory turned to the window and went deeply into thought. Two minutes passed quietly.

"Keep a lookout, David, and cable me if his condition worsens appreciably."

The months passed. Two, three, four, then with but five months wanting to complete the year, Sir Melvin took ill. During dinner, he complained of acute gastritis, then a burning pain below the sternum. Doctor Appelby was summoned. His diagnosis was horrifying – most likely a heart attack. Sir Melvin was expected to expire before morning. I cabled Gregory at once. By the time he arrived, Sir Melvin had passed on.

"Much pain?" asked Gregory.

"Minimum."

"Oh, dash it, David. Let's not pretend. He had just five months to go. What's to become of it now?"

Before I could say anything Doctor Appelby appeared at the door of the study.

"Good morning, Gregory, nice to see you," he said.

"Hello, doctor," Gregory mumbled.

The doctor smiled. "Pity we have to renew our friendship on such a forbidding occasion."

"Yes, pity."

"What will you have me do with the body, David?"

I was thinking of the inheritance. "Oh...contact Ashland and have him make the arrangements."

The doctor turned to leave and then came back into the room, put his satchel down and stared at me with a straight, cold, medicinal look.

"You know," he said slowly, "it is possible to keep this death a secret for five months."

I felt as though I had been struck. I sat down; my thoughts eddying. What is he saying? Whatever could he....?

Gregory snapped to. "Go on," he said.

"When refrigerated, a body may keep for days, and when frozen, indefinitely," said the doctor.

Gregory began to frame a question. "But..."

"The deep freezer in the basement would be suitable," said Doctor Appelby, anticipating Gregory's question. "At the end of the five month period remove the body, allow time for it to thaw of course, set it up in bed, and fetch the coroner."

"Brilliant," exclaimed Gregory.

"Splendid," was all I could muster.

"Now if..." Gregory stopped short and whirled about. "But Stephens?"

"Oh, yes," I thought - Stephens, the manservant who had been with Sir Melvin through the ages. He would not understand.... "But something should be said to him.... Suppose you talk to him, Gregory."

"Fine, David. You help the doctor; I'll speak with Stephens."

Stephens was seated in the vestibule. "Oh, Stephens," I called, as I passed him on my way upstairs, "Mr. Clot would like to speak with you for a moment."

4

Stephens looked up, his eyes red and cheeks puffed. Without saying a word he entered the parlor and stood erect. His presence startled Gregory who was arranging his thoughts.

"Oh, Stephens - yes, yes, come in, come in," he uttered. Stephens stood at attention as Gregory started what he had rehearsed.

"Now," he said by way of introduction, "we have all sustained a severe shock this evening. No one could have thought that so energetic, so robust a man as Sir Melvin could have - a - could have expired so unexpectedly. Yes, it was quite a shock. But it is in times like these that one must remain steadfast, one must --."

Thump, thump, thump. My footsteps and Doctor Appelby's, heavy and uncertain, echoed through the parlor. Stephens, unmoved, stared blankly ahead. Gregory continued.

"Yes, it is in times like these that one must ----."

Thump, thump, thump. The doctor and I, with Sir Melvin's body sprawled upon a makeshift stretcher between us, excused ourselves and passed through the parlor to the storage room. Without a word, Stephens wilted and sat down.

We eased the body into the freezer, being careful not to disarrange the nightclothes terribly. Except for one foot, it fit devilishly well.

"Had better dial it as low as possible," advised the doctor.

"Right," added Gregory with a dash of adventure.

****

My next cablegram to Gregory was five months later. "Gregory Clot, Topsworthy, stop, frightful news, stop, Sir Melvin dead, stop, come quickly, stop, David."

"Have you notified the coroner as yet?" asked Gregory.

"He will be here in a very few minutes," I answered.

The coroner arrived, extended his sympathies and explained that whereas this was death due to an unknown cause, an autopsy must be performed. We understood and agreed.

At a quarter past eleven, much to our surprise, the coroner appeared at the door.

"Come in, come in," Gregory begged.

"The hour is late, I will not detain you," said the coroner. "Sir Melvin died of a heart attack - a coronary occlusion."

"What a pity," moaned Gregory. "He was such a robust man. Riding, hunting, tennis, there seemed to be no activity foreign to Sir Melvin. That's why it's so difficult to believe he was stricken so violently and quickly. At first it appeared to be merely gastritis. Why...."

The coroner interrupted. "Then you were here at the time, Mr. Clot?"

Gregory took the cigarette from his mouth and flicked the ashes from it.

"Why - why - no, Mr. Whenton...," he said feebly, pointing to me.

"Yes," I said quickly. "Sir Melvin complained of a slight pain. It was just after dessert. We were about to...."

"Ah yes, dessert," said the coroner, squinting his eyes inquiringly, "that's one thing that bothers us, Mr. Whenton."

I glanced quickly to Gregory.

"Upon examining the stomach," the coroner said, "I found remains of fresh strawberries. Fresh strawberries in January?"

The coroner looked at me. I looked at Gregory. Gregory took a few seconds to regain his composure then straightened up and smiled - the situation well in hand.

"Yes, well, you see," he said, "we have a deep freezer."

The End

After Miranda, What?

Do you remember where you were on the 13th of June, 1966? I do. I was driving across the United States trying to get to New Jersey for a vacation. It was somewhere in Kansas when I heard it – "This is a bulletin. The United States Supreme Court today has struck down all confessions given without a lawyer present. A spokesman for the Court has said the Court held in a case from Arizona that any confession given without the defendant first being warned that he has a right to a lawyer is constitutionally invalid. We repeat...." It was the Miranda decision.

At that time I was the Chief Deputy in the Pima County Attorney's office in Tucson, Arizona. My office prosecuted hundreds of criminal cases a year. That bulletin sent us into a dither for weeks. We couldn't begin to guess what was coming next...Jails were unconstitutional? Punishment was unconstitutional? We were ready to believe almost anything.

So, in the midst of all this I wrote a fake United States Supreme Court opinion, sneaked it into the office, and sat back and waited for people to read it. I thought a few would see it, laugh, and then pass it on. But they didn't; they read it but no one saw the joke. They believed it. I was so embarrassed I didn't tell anybody until the next day.

Here it is; see what you think.

SUPREME COURT OF THE UNITED STATES
No. 615 - October Term, 1966
Benedict Di Gerlando, Petitioner,

v.

The State of New York

*On Writ of Certiorari to the
Court of Appeals of New York
State of New York,*

Per Curiam opinion of the Court.

Petitioner DiGerlando has filed a petition for habeas corpus in the Federal District Court asserting that his conviction for burglary in the New York Courts is invalid because based upon evidence improperly before the trial court in violation of petitioner's right to counsel under the 14th Amendment. The writ was denied, 208 F. Supp. 864 (D.C.S.D.N.Y.), the Court of

Appeals affirmed, 310 F.2d 271 (C.A. 2d Cir.) and we granted certiorari.

The fundamental question for our consideration is whether the admission into evidence of the officers clandestine observations constituted a denial of "the Assistance of Counsel in violation of the Sixth Amendment to the Constitution as made obligatory upon the States by the Fourteenth Amendment," Gideon v. Wainwright, 372 U.S. 335, 342.

On the night of January 19, 1964 Albany City Police received information from a "reliable" informer that the next night (that of January 20, 1964) there was to be a burglary of a fur shop in the downtown area of the city. Petitioner, the informer related, had been planning the burglary with another (one Vandettio) for approximately three days.[1] Based upon this "reliable" information the burglary squad of the Albany City Police organized what was referred to in the evidence as a "stake-out." Eight officers were selected for this purpose; all carefully picked, all made familiar with the floor plan of the fur shop, the area immediately surrounding the fur shop and the "mug shots" of petitioner and Vandettio. Two other officers set up an immediate "around-the-clock" surveillance of petitioner's apartment, noting the ingress and egress of every questionable person. Vandettio was seen to enter and leave petitioner's apartment building twice within an eight hour period immediately preceding the burglary of the fur shop. Each time Vandettio was carrying a large brown paper bag.[2]

At approximately 1:30 on the morning of January 21,1964 two surveillance officers saw a dark 1957 Chevrolet automobile stop in a parking lot a few blocks from the fur shop. Two figures were seen to leave the car and pass into an alley which, the officers later testified, led to the rear door of the fur shop. The two officers followed the figures to the rear of the shop, watched as they apparently looked about for a watchman, and then saw them enter through a small window after noiselessly breaking the pane. By means of a portable pocket radio two more officers were summoned and took their places outside the front door to the fur shop. Officers Haynes and Schroeder stood their positions and watched as the two figures entered the fur shop and moved about inside.[3] Officer Schroeder testified that after watching the figures move about for a very few minutes:

> One, the large one, came running out the back door
> and he had something that I could see was large and bulky

8

on his back. He was holding it with both of his hands and he came running right toward me. I drew my gun, shined my flashlight on him and told him to stop.... He stopped and put his hands up and when he did that he dropped the coats and just stood there....[4]

And further:

Oh, Yes, I recognized him all right. It was the defendant, Mr. DiGerlando, the man sitting right there. I identified myself and asked him who he was and what he was doing. All he would do was give me his name, Benedict DiGerlando. Well, when I picked up the fur coats I found the pipe wrapped with cloth. That was right to the left of Mr. DiGerlando.[5]

Petitioner's objection to all of Officer Schroeder's testimony from the minute he spotted petitioner until he exited was overruled by the trial court. Petitioner was convicted of burglary and he appealed the conviction. The Court of Appeals affirmed, holding that Officer Schroeder's clandestine observations did not infringe upon petitioner's constitutional right to the assistance of counsel.

At this late date it stands too well settled to admit of much reiteration that the 6th and 14th Amendments provide a formidable standard of basic fairness to all accused of crime. The right to advice and guidance of counsel is basic and all encompassing. It exists not only at the "earliest possible need" but by all concepts of due process at the "initial involvement." Spano v. New York, 360 U.S. 315 at 326 (Douglas, J. Concurring). Time and again this Court has been called upon to exercise a just restraint upon the ubiquitous and sometimes officious hand of law enforcement, Weeks v. United States, 232 U.S. 383, Mallory v. United States, 357 U.S. 261, Elkins v. United States, 361 U.S. 548, Massiah v. United States, 382 U.S. 176, Escobedo v. Illinois, 365 U.S. 902, and to see to it that an accused's right to counsel was implemented at all possible levels where his personal liberty was or may have been endangered. Such a right is not a mere pittance to be used as desired and dispensed with at will; its terms are obligatory; its scope wide.

In Massiah v. United States, 323 U.S. 233, this Court observed that "a Constitution which guarantees a defendant the aid of counsel at trial could surely vouchsafe no less to an indicted defendant...in a completely extrajudicial proceeding.... Anything less... might deny a defendant effective representation by counsel at the only stage when legal aid and advice would help him." Id. at 243 quoting Douglas, J., concurring in Spano v. United States, 360 U.S. 315, 326. It is at the earliest possible opportunity, when counsel's guidance has its greatest effect, that this right must be preserved, not at the latest possible time. Crooker v. California, 357 U.S. 433, recognized that time as the stage when "legal aid and advice are most critical to petitioner." Also see Massiah v United States, supra, at 245. Can there be room for speculation that when Benedict DiGerlando entered that fur shop he had entered a stage "when legal aid and advice" are most critical; there was possibly no more critical a stage than that very moment when the full force and implementation of the law was about to take effect, when investigation ceased and accusation began, when petitioner's liberty was arrested. Petitioner, a layman, was undoubtedly unaware of police methods and surveillance. He had no reason to suspect that his privacy belonged to anyone other than himself at that very moment. The "guiding hand of counsel" was essential to advise petitioner of his rights in this delicate situation. Powell v. Alabama, 237 U.S. 45, 69. This was most assuredly "a critical stage." Massiah v. United States, supra, at 26. It was a stage surely as critical as the arraignment in Hamilton v. Alabama, 368 U.S. 52, and the preliminary hearing in White v. Maryland, 373 U.S. 59. What happened at this stage would certainly "affect the whole trial," Hamilton v. Alabama, supra at 54, since rights "may be as irretrievably lost, if not then and there asserted, as they are when an accused represented by counsel waives a right for strategic purposes." Ibid. It would exalt form over substance to make the right to counsel, as the State of New York contends, depend upon whether at the time of the interrogation, the authorities had secured a complaint. Petitioner had, for all practical purposes, already been charged with burglary for Officer Schroeder testified that under no circumstances would he not have affected an arrest. [6] The Solicitor General, in his brief and oral argument, suggests that this Court, by its holdings, never intended the "right to counsel" to protect the observed acts of a defendant unaided by counsel but that our recent holdings prohibit only the admission of defendant's statements uttered without benefit of counsel.[7] The 6th and 14th Amendments do not strike so hollow; their protection is real, not imaginary, not illusory or subtle. Neither logic nor reason dictates a meaningful difference between that spoken and that done; each is equally incriminating; each is subject to observation. This argument proposes a difference without meaning which we decline to follow.

10

If the rule we announce today is to have any efficacy at all it must apply to indirect and surreptitious intrusions as well as to those accomplished in the public square. In this case DiGerlando was more seriously imposed upon than either Massiah or Escobedo because he did not know that he was under observation by a government agent.

There is necessarily a direct relationship between the importance of a stage to the police in their quest for a conviction and the criticalness of that stage to the accused in his need for legal advice. Our Constitution, unlike others, strikes the balance in favor of the right of the accused to be advised by his lawyer of his Constitutional rights. As we said in Escobedo, supra, at 654.

> No system worth preserving should have to fear that if an accused is permitted to consult with a lawyer, he will become aware of, and exercise these rights. If the exercise of constitutional rights will thwart the effectiveness of a system of law enforcement, then there is something very wrong with that system.

Nothing we have said today affects the powers of the police to investigate an unsolved crime by gathering information from witnesses and by other proper investigative efforts. We hold only that when the process shifts from investigatory to accusatory - when its focus is on the accused and its purpose is to elicit a confession - our adversary system begins to operate, and, under circumstances like these, the accused must be afforded advice and guidance of his lawyer.

The judgment of the New York Court of Appeals is reversed and the case remanded for proceedings not inconsistent with this opinion.

Footnotes

1 The "informer" was never identified. Officer Graham testified that he had known the informer for a number of years, that he had spoken with him on many cases and that much of the information he supplied had led to arrests in the past.

2. The contents or significance of the "brown paper bag" was never made known.

3. There was considerable doubt as to whether either of these two officers could actually see any movement at all. Officer Schroeder

testified that there was a stream of light "that appeared to be shining all the way through the shop from out in front of the shop."

4. The coats Officer Schroeder referred to were identified at trial by him and established by the owner as coming from the burglarized fur shop.

5. The State apparently contended that the pipe was the instrument used to break the pane of glass that led directly to the entry of the burglars.

6. See People v. Davis, 13 N. Y.2d 690, 191 N.E. 2d 674, 241 N.Y. L. 2d (1963); People v. Rodriguez, 11 N.Y.2d 279, 133 N.E. 2d 651, 229 N.Y.L.2d 353 (1962).

7. See Broeder, Wong Sun v. United States, A Study in Faith and Hope, 42 Neb.L.Rev. 483. "The rule sought by the State would provide a very hollow constitutional guarantee because for all practical purposes the conviction is already assured by pretrial examination. The Soviet Criminal Code does not permit a lawyer to be present during the investigation. The Soviet trial has thus been aptly described as an 'appeal from the pretrial investigation.' " Feifer, "Justice in Moscow" (1964), 86.

Schmid

"Four Tucson Teenage Girls Have Disappeared Into Thin Air"
[Nov. 4, 1965, the Tucson Daily Star]

"Police detectives frankly admit they have no idea where they have gone." The mothers of all four girls were afraid that something bad had happened to them and two mothers insisted their daughters were dead. One of the girls was Alleen Rowe, a pretty 15 year old Palo Verde High School sophomore. A year before the article, her mother, a nurse, went to work on the night shift and when she got home the next morning Alleen was gone. She called the school and a number of friends but no one had seen her that day. Then she called the police.

[The fate of one of the four missing girls is not known and is not part of this story.]

At the time of this story I was the Chief Deputy Pima County Attorney in Tucson.

Three months before the Daily Star article, Gretchen Fritz, who was 16, and her sister, Wendy, 14, the daughters of Dr. and Mrs. James M. Fritz, left home in Gretchen's car saying they were going to a movie at the Cactus Drive-In Theater. The car was found the next day parked at a local motel, keys still in the ignition and Gretchen's purse on the front seat.

The police questioned friends of the missing girls and published dozens of circulars with pictures of them asking for help in finding them. But they got no worthwhile results. There were a number of calls from people who thought they saw them in Tucson, in Phoenix, some surrounding towns, Mexico and other states, but they led nowhere. Mrs. Rowe talked to the police a number of times and every time she told them they should speak to a boy named Schmid, a friend of his named Saunders and a girlfriend named French because she was sure they knew something about Alleen's disappearance. And the police did talk to them, all three more than once, but they said they knew nothing about her disappearance.

"It is possible," said a detective, "that one or all of the girls could be victims of foul play," but he was "inclined to believe that they were still alive." "There are thousands of reasons why teenagers run away or leave home," he said, "and we have absolutely nothing to indicate that these girls' lives were in danger."

Then about a year after the Daily Star article, a Tucson man named Bruns called the Tucson police. He said his son, Richie, who was living in Ohio temporarily at his grandmother's house, knew who murdered the Fritz sisters and Alleen Rowe, and he knew where the bodies were buried. If the police would pay his way back to Tucson he would show them where they were buried.

13

The father said that a year ago a man named Charles Schmid told Richie that he killed Alleen Rowe and he took him to the spot where he buried her in the desert east of Tucson. To prove to Richie that a body was buried there Schmid poked a stick into the ground to show that the ground was soft and when he pulled the stick out there was a putrid smell. Schmid told him he also killed the Fritz sisters because he told the oldest sister, Gretchen, that he killed Alleen and he was afraid she would tell the police. He said he had to kill Wendy because she was with her sister that night. He also took Bruns to the spot where he disposed of the bodies of the Fritz sisters in shallow graves in the desert hills north of Tucson.

Immediately a Tucson city Police detective flew to Columbus and brought Bruns back. When they got off the plane in Tucson that night they took him to a desert area off of Pontatoc Road north of Tucson where Schmid said he buried the Fritz sisters. It was dark and Bruns wasn't sure he had the right place but once he spotted the radio towers he told the police they should start searching. They found scattered bones, a skull, bits of clothing, shoes, shorts, jeans, and a girl's blouse, but Bruns believed there was more because the bodies were not buried very deeply and animals had uncovered them and scattered bones and clothing over a wide area. They continued their search in the morning and they found a few more articles of clothing and dark stains on the ground that smelled like body fluids. Everything was photographed, put into plastic bags and taken to the mortuary. The remains were identified by Mrs. Fritz and the coroner as those of her daughters.

When this took place Charles Schmid was 23, all of his friends and the three girls he killed were teenagers and they followed him and did whatever he told them to do. A book written after the trials called him "The Pied Piper of Tucson." He was a good-looking young man, but he was different. He had been a high school gymnastics champion, he was very polite, he was mannerly, he spoke well, and the mothers of his teenage friends liked him. He also dyed his hair, wore pancake make-up, put axle grease on his face for a beauty mark, wore a metal bridge on his nose pretending he had been injured, and at various times told his friends he had incurable cancer. He always carried tiny bottles of salt and pepper with which, he told friends, he used to blind opponents, and he liked to impress friends with "highfalutin" language like, "I can manifest my neurotical (sic) emotions, emancipate an epicureal (sic) instinct, and elaborate on my heterosexual tendencies." A second grade teacher said "He was an overly curious boy. He was brighter than most but seemed to be interested in what he wanted to be interested in."

He stood 5 feet 3 inches but with his boots on he was three inches taller. He was very conscious of his height and he stuffed rags, cans, and cardboard in his boots to make him taller. And he practiced walking in the boots.

He had been adopted as an infant and his adopted mother gave him a house in Tucson next to hers. She also paid for all of his bills, carried meals to him, gave him an allowance of $300 a month, cleaned his house, and let him lead his own life. He had no job and only occasional duties around his house. Friends told him he looked like Elvis Pressley and he agreed. He wanted to play the guitar, sing like Elvis, and make a record. He messed around with a guitar, but never learned to play it. He did, however, pretend to play it in front of his friends with a record player hidden behind him. The Tucson Citizen newspaper called him a "strutting braggart."

Schmid's girlfriend at the time was Mary French, a teenager who dropped out of high school. Not many of the kids liked her. She was a "frump with a lumpy face," "a cold cookie, a dead fish," "a hostile, young lady, silent and sullen," and "her body was shapeless." When I interviewed her in the jail right after her arrest she sat across from me at a small metal table and talked to my eyes the whole time. She frightened me; she was cold and harsh and I made sure that a deputy sheriff was standing just a few feet away.

John Saunders, another high school dropout, was a close friend of Schmid. He was a teenager, "a poor student and constantly in minor trouble," not very smart, slow and quiet, and he followed Schmid's lead.

On May 30, 1964 Schmid told Mary French that he wanted to kill a girl to see what it was like and to see "if he could get away with it." He asked Mary to pick a victim. When she couldn't think of anyone he suggested they choose one of three girls he had in mind. Mary called two of them; "one of them was a wrong number and the other was busy" so that left the third one, Alleen Rowe. She lived with her single mother and two brothers just a few houses away from Mary French. Her mother tried to keep a tight rein on her and told her she thought Mary French and Schmid were bad influences.

Mary French didn't like Alleen and being the last one on the list she called her and asked her to go out that night with her, Schmid and John Saunders. Schmid had a car and she said they would go out into the desert and have a party. But Alleen said no, she had to baby-sit that night for a neighbor. Mary called the neighbor's house and again asked her to go with them, but Alleen refused. When Mary called a third time Alleen said okay, but they would have to wait until her mother went to work; then she would slip out the back door and meet them.

About midnight that night, after they had circled the neighborhood to make sure that Mrs. Rowe's car was gone, Schmid parked his car in an alley near the Rowe house and Mary got out and tapped on Alleen's bedroom window. In a few minutes Alleen came out the back door in a bathing suit and shift and curlers in her hair.

Schmid drove to a desert area east of Tucson with Mary in the front seat with him and John Saunders in the back with Alleen. He parked and while he and Mary stayed in the car Saunders and Alleen walked into the desert. Within minutes they heard a scream from Alleen and Schmid told Mary to wait in the car and he took off into the desert.

When he reached Saunders and Alleen they took off Alleen's bathing suit and tied her hands with a guitar string Schmid had with him. Schmid told Saunders to go ahead and rape her, but Saunders couldn't do it. So Schmid did while Saunders wandered off and smoked a cigarette. When he returned, Alleen was adjusting the straps on her bathing suit and Schmid grabbed a large rock and hit her on the head. She started to run and he ran after her and hit her again. This time she fell to the ground, her head bleeding. Schmid ran back to the car, very excited. "We killed her," he told Mary and he told her to get the shovel out of the back of the car.

All three dug a hole with the shovel and their hands, put Alleen's body in it and covered it with sand. Then they collected Alleen's hair curlers that were scattered about and Mary dug a hole with her hands and placed them in it. As they left, Schmid told them to tell no one.

Two months after that, Schmid spotted a young blonde girl at a public swimming pool. Later that day, he collected some used pots from his house and took them to the girl's house and pretended he had pots to sell her. The blonde was Gretchen Fritz, a teenager and the daughter of a Tucson heart surgeon. She had a younger sister named Wendy.

During the next few months Schmid and Gretchen were with each other most of the time. They made love often and argued often. At one point Schmid told Gretchen that years before he had killed a boy, cut off his hands, buried him in the desert, and recorded it all in a diary. The police never found a diary, none of the kids had ever seen a diary and to this day a diary has never turned up. Schmid also told her that he killed Alleen Rowe and offered to take her out to show her the body but Gretchen refused to go.

All the time Schmid was with Gretchen he had other girls. Gretchen knew it and it wasn't long before she became very jealous and told him that if he didn't stop seeing them she would tell her father and the police about the boy he killed, about killing Alleen Rowe, and the diary. To cement that threat she stole his diary.

More than a year after the murder of Alleen Rowe, Gretchen and Wendy went to a drive-in movie in Gretchen's Pontiac Lemans. They never came home and the car was found four days later at a local motel. The driver's seat had been pushed back, the speedometer was

16

disconnected, there was gravel and mud on the floor, and Gretchen's keys and her purse with $20 dollars in it were in the car. Schmid had strangled the sisters, buried them in the desert off Pontatoc Road north of Tucson and ditched Gretchen's car. He told Bruns he was proud of it.

In November of 1965 Richard Bruns got into trouble. He was convicted of disorderly conduct involving his girlfriend and her father. He didn't want anyone seeing his girlfriend and he kept watch on her house to make sure no one went near her. At one point he armed himself with a baseball bat and stationed himself in a tree in the front yard and in various other places around the house. The girl's father filed criminal charges against him in the Tucson city court. He was convicted and placed on probation for six months and ordered to spend the first three months with his grandmother in Ohio. When he got to Ohio he was bored, he had nothing to do, no one to do anything with and he missed his girlfriend. He couldn't stand it and he was afraid Schmid might do something to his girlfriend so he called his father and told him that he wanted to turn Schmid in, knowing that that would get him back to Tucson - and of course it did. Once back in Tucson he took the police to the remains of the Fritz sisters and to where he thought Alleen Rowe was buried but he couldn't find the spot. He didn't know that after Schmid showed him the spot Schmid dug up the body and reburied it because he was afraid Bruns might go to the police.

Even though we couldn't find Alleen's body we filed a murder charge against all three for killing Alleen and two separate murder charges against Schmid for killing the Fritz sisters. Schmid was arrested at his home in Tucson, French was arrested in Texas, and Saunders was arrested in Connecticut. Immediately after their arrests all three were arraigned in a justice court in a very brief appearance; just long enough to tell them what they were charged with, to ask if they had attorneys, and to allow them to ask for bail. Bail was denied and lawyers were appointed for French and Saunders. Schmid's lawyer, Bill Tinney, was hired by his mother and he asked the magistrate to keep everyone out of the court except the attorneys and the defendants but the magistrate denied the request. After that short hearing, Schmid was taken to the police station and with reporters present taking notes and photos he was asked to take off his boots and dump the contents on the floor. He did and in the boots were "folded up rags flattened beer cans, which were covered over with a wadding of more rags and pieces of cardboard."

While this was going on the police were executing a search warrant at Schmid's house. They examined everything, even the crawl space under the house. They were looking for anything that would back up Bruns' story, especially a guitar string that Schmid told Bruns he used to strangle Gretchen. They found a guitar minus one string but no loose strings, or anything else that would bolster Bruns' story.

The County attorney and I decided our case was not very strong if none of the three decided to talk. Bruns would be our only witness and we didn't believe that with his background, the jury would find him credible. Bruns was an unusual looking fellow, 6 feet tall, very skinny, weighed 102 pounds, had spent 2 years in Fort Grant, the prison for juveniles, for burglary, had read one book in his life, *Dracula*, attended a number of schools and quit all of them. Some of Schmid's friends called him a "misfit." So we decided to offer French or Saunders a plea agreement in return for their testimony against Schmid. Unfortunately, the County Attorney, who had never practiced criminal law, made the offer to both attorneys, thinking he would take the first one who agreed. But their lawyers were experienced and they both accepted the offers at the same time. We believed that ethically we were bound to accept both of them – and we did. The agreement was that in exchange for testimony against Schmid and for showing the police where the body of Alleen was buried, Mary French would get 5 years in prison and Saunders would get a life sentence. Once they signed the agreements, each of them took the police to the desert where they remembered burying Alleen, but they couldn't find the spot. All they could find were the curlers Mary French had buried. That was not good for our case. That would hurt the credibility of French and Saunders because they both told the police that Alleen was buried next to the curlers.

Finding someone in the desert is not an easy job. We, the Sheriff's department, the police, and a number of citizens never stopped searching, but we found nothing. Then one day I got a message at the office from a woman in Mesa who said her grandfather was a diviner, a person who finds things under the ground with a wooden stick. If we thought he could help he was willing to come to Tucson, she said. Well, that sounded very interesting but I was afraid the press would hear about it and they would make us look like fools - looking for a dead body with a stick? And I had little faith that the old man would find anything. But if we didn't take the risk we would probably get criticized for not doing everything we could do to find the body. I decided it would be worth the risk and I told one of my investigators to go to Mesa, get the man and take him to where we thought the body might be buried - but to make sure no one knew what he was doing. The investigator picked him up in Mesa very early the next morning. The old man had a long stick with him with a string tied on the end and a small bone tied to the end of the string, just like a fishing pole with a fly on the end. The investigator drove to the area where we thought the body might be but then kept on going, past the place Mary French and John Saunders had pointed out. The old man told him to stop and to back up; he said they had passed the area where the body was. They went back and the old man walked into the desert with his long stick held in front of him. He told the investigator the bone would twirl when it found the body. And the bone did twirl a bit but it never found the body. And the press never heard about it.

So, I had to prepare to try a first degree murder case without the victim's body, a most unusual predicament, one that I had only read about happening in other places. In my research I could find only three cases in the world where a murder charge was successfully prosecuted without a body.

Within a few weeks we went to court for a preliminary hearing against Schmid for the murders of the Fritz sisters. A hearing for the murder of Alleen would come later. Preliminary hearings in Arizona are held in a Justice Court where the "judge" is a person who won the last election as Justice of the Peace and doesn't have to be a lawyer. The hearings are supposed to be short and to the point – the point being to put on just enough evidence to show that a crime was committed and the person in custody is probably the person who committed it. Murder cases are different, however. They are usually contentious affairs, the defense is trying to find out everything it can about the state's case and the state is trying to prevent that from happening. The Schmid-Fritz hearing was contentious. It lasted six days and produced 464 pages of transcript. I put on the stand only a handful of witnesses to describe the murder scene and identify the bodies, Bruns, and the coroner, just enough to show that Gretchen and Wendy were murdered and Schmid was probably the one who did it. Mr. Tinney cross-examined each of them extensively. I did not put on either Mary French or John Saunders because neither was needed. When I finished, Mr. Tinney put on 13 witnesses, including Mary French and John Saunders trying to find out what other evidence the state had. But with their attorneys present they both invoked their 5th Amendment rights and refused to testify. That ended the hearing and the Justice of the Peace ordered that Schmid be held for trial in the Superior Court on both charges. Then, out in the hallway, the justice, surrounded by the press and still in his rust-colored robe, was asked what he thought about the state's case. He said he had trouble with it because it was "not one of the best cases in the world, in fact it's one of the worst." That was a rather silly thing for him to say because he had heard only a fraction of the state's case. He knew that and so did the press and fortunately they made nothing of it. He was quoted in the newspaper the next morning but it was not mentioned again and I was not asked to comment on it.

The preliminary hearing on the Alleen Rowe murder took place three weeks later. Both French and Saunders testified and Schmid was held to answer to the murder charge in Superior Court.

John Sanders pleaded guilty to first degree murder and was sentenced to prison for life and Mary French pleaded guilty to being an accessory to a murder and concealing and compounding a felony and received 4 to 5 years in prison.

The publicity surrounding the case was intense. Life Magazine did a feature story on the case with a picture on the cover of Schmid being arrested in his boots and with his make-up on, Playboy Magazine sent a reporter to cover the proceedings, almost everything that happened was covered by national TV and radio, and everybody connected with the case was in the newspapers for months. Because of this, Superior Court Judge Richard Roylston, entered a gag order on November 23, 1965, at the request of Schmid's attorney and over my objection, muzzling all law enforcement agencies. We were not allowed to talk to the media about any aspect of the cases. Tucson's afternoon newspaper summed it up by printing that, "in effect, Judge Roylston put the news media on probation." The order of course, caused the nation's press to boil; they said it was unconstitutional and they threatened lawsuits. But the gag order stayed intact and the question of the constitutionality of gag orders was not decided until 10 years later by the United States Supreme Court in a different case.

Schmid's attorney filed a motion to have the cases moved to federal court, he filed a motion to continue the trials, and a motion to have the trials moved to another county, and all were denied. But the state did not fare that well when the judge set dates for each trial. I wanted Schmid to be tried for the Rowe murder first. That way, assuming he was convicted of killing her, it would be difficult for him to convince a jury at the Fritz trial that he had no motive for killing the sisters. But the judge set the Fritz trial first, to begin on February 15, 1966.

My theory of the case followed the story Richard Bruns told; Schmid killed Gretchen and Wendy Fritz because Gretchen was threatening to tell the police about the Rowe murder and Schmid's diary and Gretchen just happened to be with her that night. With the Fritz trial first, I would have to prove not only the murders of the sisters but also the murder of Alleen Rowe.

Proving crimes committed by a defendant other than the one he is charged with is not easy to do and it is not done very often, especially in a murder case. In a court of law it isn't relevant that the defendant killed before. It is relevant, however, if the prior murder was a reason for the later killing - and here it was. I prepared a legal memo on the admissibility of evidence of another crime and filed it before the trial started and the judge agreed with me, evidence of Alleen's murder would be admitted to help prove the murders of the Fritz sisters.

Once the deaths were established at trial and the remains identified as the Fritz sisters by hair, teeth and clothing Mary French testified about the murder of Alleen Rowe. Saunders was to be the next witness but when he was called to the stand he surprised everyone by refusing to testify. He said he stood on his constitutional right not to testify and I did not try to force him to. We never found out why he did that.

Richard Bruns testified to seeing the mutilated bodies of the Fritz sisters and that Schmid confessed to all three murders. Schmid did not testify and the jury convicted him of both murders and he was sentenced to death for each.

Although the trial of the Rowe case was set to begin a few weeks later, Schmid's attorney moved to continue it because of the intense publicity. The judge agreed and he continued the trial until October 1966. With the delay, Schmid's attorney called an old Marine buddy of his, a nationally prominent criminal trial attorney named F. Lee Bailey, who was becoming one of the best known defense attorneys in the country. He had successfully defended Dr. Sam Sheppard in the United States Supreme Court and got his conviction for murdering his wife reversed and then won him an acquittal at the retrial. He went on from there to defend Dr. Coppolino in Florida against a charge of murdering his wife, Ernest Medina on murder charges at the My Lai massacre in Viet Nam, Patty Hearst who was kidnapped by the Symbionese Army in California and eventually helped them rob a bank, and Albert DeSalvo, the Boston strangler. Mr.Tinney asked Bailey, who lived in Boston, to come out to Arizona and co-chair the defense for Schmid. Bailey said he would think about it.

Then Schmid himself filed a petition to have the court order a lie detector test to prove his innocence (he told the press he would be willing to have Dr. Fritz administer the serum). That was denied. He also filed a motion to have a different attorney. He wanted Percy Foreman, one of the most prominent criminal defense attorneys at the time. Foreman suggested F. Lee Bailey, telling Schmid: "He's a young man, probably the second best attorney in the country, very aggressive." He never said who the best attorney in the country was.

With that prompting, Bailey told the national press that he was interested in the Schmid case and that he would fly to Tucson and talk to Schmid at the state prison. He wondered aloud to the press why Schmid had not taken the stand at the Fritz trial and why there had been no psychiatric testimony. Mr. Tinney told him why: "there had been psychiatric examinations, and the results would scare the pants off any lawyer." Bailey suggested a private lie detector test to be administered by one of his assistants, and then he left town on his Lear jet saying he wouldn't take the case unless Schmid passed the test.

Well, Schmid must have passed the test because two weeks later Bailey said he would take the case, but Schmid would have to also retain Mr. Tinney.

A defense fund was set up but it raised only $36.

Schmid was pleased with Bailey and he told the press: "Mr. Bailey told me, 'Charlie, I don't know whether you'll be out of here next summer or 11 years from now, but you'll be out.' "

Bailey asked for another trial continuance telling the judge "An article a day keeps justice away." He lost that motion, but shortly before the October trial date he made a motion in the federal district court to have the trial moved to federal court. The district judge delayed the trial for a few days but after a hearing he denied the motion. The trial was reset for April 3, then it was reset again for May 10, 1967. In the meantime, Schmid and Bailey kept talking to the press. Schmid whined about how unfair the system was, how expensive it was, and that he was sure I was afraid to face Bailey in court. Over his favorite radio station he said: "When Mr. Bailey and one of the most qualified polygraph experts administered me a polygraph examination, they telephoned Mr. Schafer and asked him to be present before they gave the test, and he flatly refused. And he also flatly refused to accept the results of that test. I can only guarantee you one thing, and one thing only, I'll never give up."

The trial began on May 10, 1967 with Judge Richard Roylston calling 125 prospective jurors. It took a number of days to winnow that down to 12 jurors and 3 alternates. Bailey made a motion to prevent the jury from considering a death sentence because the body of Ms. Rowe had not been found. The judge denied the motion. Then he asked the court to prevent the state from offering evidence of other murders, the murders of the Fritz sisters. The judge denied that. He then moved to have the trial delayed and be moved to another county and that was denied. Then he said he had one final motion. He asked the court to rule that it had no jurisdiction to go ahead with a trial against "a man who is, under the law as I read it, already legally dead." The judge thought it was an interesting point, but he denied the motion.

Bailey then questioned the prospective jurors about their ability to be fair. First he asked if any of them thought Schmid was guilty because he was represented by F. Lee Bailey. No one answered yes. Then he spent time emphasizing the fact that the body of the victim had never been found. He told them it would not do if they believed that the victim was probably dead. He said "We don't use probabilities. So long as there is a possibility that the alleged victim might turn up somewhere would you be inclined to vote for the death penalty - or hold up?"

Before the trial started I had called a few prosecutors who had faced Bailey in court to find out what to expect. They said he was very smart, quick, used his voice very well, commanded attention, and could be tricky. As an example, one of them told me a story that didn't involve Bailey but did involve the murder of a young girl whose body was never found. When that defense attorney gave his closing argument to the jury he talked about the fact that there was no body and asked the jurors how they could convict someone knowing that possibly the so-called victim was not dead. Then quickly he turned toward the courtroom door and, pointing at it, shouted "There she is now." Everyone turned toward the door. There was nobody there and the attorney looked at the jurors, "See, he said, "not even you believe she's dead." But the prosecutor was unmoved and when he got up to make his rebuttal argument he said to the jury, "Everybody in the courtroom looked toward the door except for one person - the defendant – because he knows she's dead."

Oh, my Lord, that was clever, probably not true, but I could see Bailey using that on the jury - and I could see myself being prepared for it.

But we never got that far.

Neither Mr. Bailey nor Mr. Tinney made an opening statement and I called the state's first witness – Alleen Rowe's mother. Bailey asked her no questions.

Mary French was the next witness. Once again she told the story of the murder. Bailey's cross-examination was short, only about 20 minutes and right to the point. Once he finished making his points, that Mary hated Alleen Rowe and that she was more than a mere stand-by at the murder; she was one of the instigators, and that she was lying about Schmid's involvement because he refused to marry her when she told him she was pregnant, Bailey stopped, "That's all," he said, and sat down.

I was about to call John Saunders as the next witness hoping that he reconsidered his decision not to testify but his attorney asked that we meet in the judge's chambers first. When we got there he said that Saunders would again take the 5th Amendment and not testify. Knowing he would do that I could not ethically put him on the stand and have him do it in front of the jury. Instead I moved to introduce the transcript of his testimony at the Rowe preliminary hearing and I filed a legal memo saying that was proper. Bailey was surprised and said he had not anticipated it and had not done any research on that point. He asked for some time to do research. The judge said he was inclined to agree with the State and would allow the transcript to be read, but he would take a 15 minute recess to let the defense do research. Bailey smiled and asked for more time: "Your Honor, my law professors would shudder to think that such an important point would be allotted only 15 minutes for research." To which the judge replied: "Mr. Bailey, that's why you had law professors, to teach you how to look up things you needed in a hurry."

After the recess, to the surprise of just about everyone in the courtroom, Bailey announced that Schmid would plead guilty to murder in the second degree, if the state would agree. I agreed and Schmid pleaded guilty and admitted in open court that he killed Alleen Rowe.

Judge Roylston: "Do you desire to enter this plea, Mr. Schmid? Schmid: " Yes."

"Have any promises been made to you: No."

"Have any threats been made to you: No."

"Is this a voluntary plea: Yes."

"Are you pleading because you are guilty or for some other reason?"

"Because I am guilty."

As Bailey was leaving the courtroom, he leaned over my shoulder and said "You know there's another one out there, don't you?" I nodded "yes," sure that he meant the boy with no hands. But such a body has never been found.

After he pleaded guilty, Schmid told a different story to his family. He told his father that he didn't want to plead guilty and he was preparing a petition to dismiss both attorneys because Bailey told him that Schafer was going to bring in evidence of the Fritz murders that would destroy his appeal of the Fritz convictions and he would be dead within ninety days. Schmid said he told Bailey "Hell no! We'll win! No deal, there's no body."

Schmid filed a motion to fire his attorneys and to withdraw his plea of guilty. The judge would not allow him to withdraw his plea but he did allow him to get new attorneys and he fired Bailey and Tinney. He got a local attorney but he did very little except to guide him through the sentencing. He was sentenced to 50 years to life and he got another court-appointed lawyer to file an appeal.

Then a very curious thing happened. A month or so later, Schmid sent a message to the Sheriff that he would take him to the body of Alleen Rowe. The Sheriff called me and Judge Roylston and asked if it could be done. I said yes and so did the judge. I told the Sheriff I would go out there but not with him because I knew it would be a press parade – and that's what it was; a line of cars, led by the Sheriff in his car and the coroner in the front seat, Schmid in handcuffs in the back seat, deputy sheriff cars following and then press cars. When it reached the eastern outskirts of Tucson, Schmid had them stop the car near where French and Saunders had taken the police months before. Schmid took them to where he had reburied the body (he moved it after he and French and Saunders buried it) and the sheriff's men started digging. Schmid also dug with his hands in handcuffs. He was anxious to show everyone, he said, that Alleen's skull was not fractured and he was therefore innocent.

Just a foot or so below the surface they found the body. Schmid cleared the dirt around the skull and kept telling the coroner that when they got the skull out of the hole they would see that there was no fracture.

When the dirt was wiped away from the skull, the coroner reached in and picked it up carefully and turned it toward me. I could see what looked like a large, long split on the side of the skull.

"Although I've never seen a skull fracture before, to me that looks like one." He nodded his head and said, "Yep, a big one."

Nevertheless, Schmid stood up and said to the press "See, there's no fracture."

The body was found just 20 yards from where the old man's bone had twirled.

The End

Postcript

The Arizona Supreme Court affirmed Schmid's convictions for killing the Fritz sisters and the two death sentences and the Court of Appeals affirmed his conviction for killing Ms. Rowe and his sentence of 50 years.

Schmid sent me a letter telling me what a good job I did and asked me to be his lawyer.

When I was elected Pima County Attorney the next year he sent me a letter of congratulation.

A year later Schmid was killed at the state prison by two inmates.

Neither the Tucson Police nor the Sheriff's Department has a record of finding a body of a boy with no hands.

There were two books published about the cases: "The Pied Piper of Tucson" by Don Moser and Jerry Cohen, and "The Tucson Murders" by John Gilmore.

No one knows what happened to the $36 collected for Schmid's defense and no one knows if F. Lee Bailey got paid for his work. There was a rumor that he had an agreement with Schmid that Bailey would get the profits from the movie everyone expected to be made. That rumor was never confirmed but there was a movie. On the few occasions I saw Mr. Bailey after the case he didn't mention a movie and he didn't say whether he received any money for his efforts.

I never saw the movie or heard of anyone who did but, I met with a Hollywood producer in Tucson a number of times after the trials were over, and on my way to a speaking engagement in Louisville, Kentucky years later, a cab driver said there was a movie in town about that "famous murderer" in Tucson. Unfortunately I didn't stay long enough to see the movie and I never heard from the producer again.

Old Drum

During its 1872 July term, the Missouri Supreme Court announced what appeared to be an innocuous opinion concerning $100. The opinion started with these words: "Suit was brought originally before a justice of the peace for killing plaintiff's dog, and damages were laid at $100" and ended ten sentences later with a decision for the dog's owner. That was 106 years ago and we are still talking about the case that prompted that opinion. You may recognize it as "Senator Vest's Tribute To The Dog."

The dog was named Old Drum. He was a black hound dog and he had been Charles Burden's companion for a number of years. They lived in Warrensburg, Missouri. Burden's brother-in-law, Leonidas Hornsby, lived next door and they were both farmers.

Hornsby was having a hard time. Dogs and wolves were killing his sheep and he couldn't stop them. He vowed that he would shoot the next stray dog that appeared on his property. On October 28 Old Drum wandered onto his property. Hornsby later said that he and his nephew thought the dog might belong to a neighbor so they decided to load their gun with corn and shoot the dog with that, which would scare it, rather than kill it. The nephew did the shooting and when the dog was hit it jumped over a fence and limped away.

Charles Burden heard that shot and remembered Hornsby's threat to kill any dog that wandered onto his property. So he called his dogs home and all reported in except his favorite, Old Drum. A dog's howling could be heard through the night and during his search for Old Drum the next morning. He thought that perhaps Hornsby had shot a dog that night, but he thought it probably belonged to a neighbor named Davenport. He went to Hornsby's house and asked him if he had heard the shot and if he shot at a dog. Hornsby said he heard the shot and his nephew shot at a dog, but it was not Old Drum, he thought it was a neighbor's dog. When Burden found Old Drum's body beside a creek it looked as though someone had placed it there. A number of shots had entered its body and sorrel horse hairs were found on its body. Hornsby owned a sorrel mule. Burden filed a lawsuit against Hornsby for $100 in the Madison County Justice Court. Hornsby's lawyers then filed a motion to dismiss it because $100 was beyond the Justice Court's jurisdiction and the judge allowed Burden to amend his complaint to ask for $50, which was within the court's jurisdiction. The case went to trial and the jury couldn't reach a verdict. At the second trial the jury awarded Burden $50. Hornsby then appealed and won a new trial. At the third trial the jury gave its verdict to Hornsby.

Burden then discovered that Hornsby had removed bullets from the body of Old Drum and he moved for a new trial based on that new evidence. His motion was granted and a fourth trial was set. Burden was represented by George G. Vest who was well known in the area and later, in 1879, he was elected to the U.S. Senate from Missouri. The fourth trial began in 1870 and it took place in the Old Johnson County Courthouse in Warrensburg, before Judge Foster Wright.

When Mr. Vest made his closing argument to the jury he didn't mention the evidence or Old Drum, he used only a pocketful of sentences, and it took only a few minutes, but that is what we have remembered for more than 100 years. This is what he said:

"The best human friend a man has in this world may turn against him and become his enemy. His son or daughter that he has reared with loving care may prove ungrateful. Those who are nearest and dearest to us, those whom we trust with our happiness and our good name, may become traitors to their faith. The money that a man has, he may lose. It flies away from him, perhaps when he needs it the most. A man's reputation may be sacrificed in a moment of ill-considered action. The people who are prone to fall on their knees to do us honor when success is with us may be the first to throw the stone of malice when failure settles its cloud upon our heads. The one absolutely unselfish friend that a man can have in this selfish world, the one that never deserts him and the one that never proves ungrateful or treacherous is his dog.

"A man's dog stands by him in prosperity and in poverty, in health and in sickness. He will sleep on the cold ground, where the wintry wind blows and the snow drifts fiercely, if only he may be near his master's side. He will kiss the hand that has no food to offer. He will lick the wounds and sores that come in encounter with the roughness of the world. He guards the sleep of his pauper master as if he were a prince. When all other friends desert, he remains. When riches take wings and reputation falls to pieces, he is as constant in his love as the sun in its journey through the heavens.

"If fortune drives the master forth an outcast in the world, friendless and homeless, the faithful dog asks no higher privilege than that of accompanying him to guard against danger, to fight against his enemies, and when the last scene of all comes, and

28

when death takes the master in its embrace and his body is laid away in the cold ground, no matter if all other friends pursue their way, there by the graveside may the noble dog be found, his head between his paws, his eyes sad but open in alert watchfulness, faithful and true even to death."

Some say that before awarding Mr. Burden $50, the jury asked if they could award more money than he had asked for, but that cannot be proved.

The End

Treetop Turner and the Super-Juries

The only time I ever saw Aaron "Treetop" Turner was in 1957. I was on my way to Cincinnati and he was on his way home. I was sitting in a Pennsylvania Railroad car in Ohio and he was on the front page of the Philadelphia Inquirer waving goodbye to his lawyer on the steps of the Philadelphia City Hall; a tall, large black man, his hand in the air as if placed there by a photographer, a look of bewilderment on his face. He had been in prison for eleven years, convicted of the same murder five times and sentenced to death four times. But on October 11, 1957, he was released - a final ending in what one Pennsylvania Supreme Court justice called a "search for the priceless jewel of truth."

The law, that sort of hocus-pocus science.

December 15, 1945. Philadelphia, Pennsylvania. Christmas time. It was cold; a light snow had fallen two days before and some of it was still clogging the sewers and sticking to the clay bricks in the sidewalk. Three men moseyed about on the corner of Second and Chestnut, blowing in their hands and rubbing their arms against their bodies, every once in a while glancing toward a narrow storefront building, the Ace Broom Factory, diagonally across from them. It was getting on to six in the afternoon and the men could see a man moving about in the front end of the factory. From his movements it looked as though he was getting ready to close; picking things up, putting things back on the shelves and arranging other things for the weekend. Soon he disappeared behind something at the side of the factory and the three men on the corner huddled for a second or two.

They looked up and down the intersecting streets. They could see no one. Then very quickly, while the man in the factory was still out of sight, they crossed the street. One, Clarence Lofton, dropped behind while the other two entered the store.

The two looked about, searching for the employee and the owner. The layout of the factory was quite familiar to them and they knew that at closing time the owner, Charles Simmons, was usually in the back. They had watched the movements in the factory for more than a week and they knew that at the end of the week Mr. Simmons would be in the back counting out the week's profit and the employee, Frank Endres, would be fiddling around in the front somewhere closing up. As they started in the door, Aaron

"Treetop" Turner took a large iron sash-weight from his pants. The other man, Jasper "Playboy" Johnson stood behind him peering about the factory for either of the two men they knew were there. Then suddenly Frank Endres appeared. They startled each other and as Frank started toward them, Treetop raised the sash and hit him on the head. Frank stopped, staggered and tried to reach for something. Treetop hit him again and he dropped to the floor. "Playboy" reached into Frank's pocket, took his wallet and then he and Turner started to the rear of the factory. As they did, the rear door opened and out popped Charles Simmons, disturbed by what he had heard. "Treetop" beat him to the floor with the iron sash and then took his wallet. Within minutes all three of the robbers were in a taproom at Eighth and Callowill toasting the season.

In the wake lay two bodies, skulls crushed and pockets turned inside out. Blood had flowed into pools on the floor and had splashed against the wall and onto the straw brooms stacked and ready for Monday. Neither Endres nor Simmons ever regained consciousness; within five days both were dead and the net profit to the robbers was a little more than $200.

Shortly after ten, while Turner and his friends were drinking on Callowill Street, the Philadelphia police removed the bodies and began the long search for clues. They talked to neighbors, they talked to businessmen, and they talked to families. There was nothing, no fingerprints, no eyewitnesses, no weapon, nothing left at the scene.

Two more of Philadelphia's 200 murders a year sat on the books. For months the police processed every call, every rumor, every slight lead. But there was nothing, nothing that indicated the slightest thing about the murders except that there had been two deaths from beatings by a blunt instrument; what kind of an instrument no one knew because it was never found.

Then, in May, about five months later, something happened. All during the time since the murders the Philadelphia police had been investigating a series of other robbery-murders dating back some months and none with a peculiar pattern. None of them appeared to have any bearing, any real resemblance to the broom factory case, until the police talked to a suspect named Clarence Lofton. He was picked up on May 24, 1946, and when they talked to him about these other crimes he began to nibble at crimes the police thought were not connected with him. One of them was the murders at the Ace Broom Factory on December 15, 1945. The names that came up in the talk were "Jasper," "Fats," "Playboy"

Johnson and Aaron "Treetop" Turner. Soon after his initial conversations with the police, Lofton confessed that he, Turner and Johnson committed the Ace Broom murders.

Without warrants or complaints, "Treetop" was arrested on June 3, 1946, and "Playboy" five hours later. The police were well aware that they did not have enough evidence to convict either of the two of the murders of Endres and Simmons. All they had was Lofton's statement that he had been a "lookout" while the others went into the factory to rob the owner. This, of course, was the statement of an accomplice and in Pennsylvania that meant very little; the law required corroboration, something in addition to Lofton to show that "Treetop" and "Playboy" participated in the murders. But there was nothing. No one saw any of the three approach the broom factory that day or any other day. No one saw them leave and no one heard them discussing the robbery. There were no fingerprints, there were no telltale articles left behind by the robbers and no weapon was ever found. And, of course, there were no eyewitnesses - both of them were dead.

When Detective Daniel O'Mahoney arrested Turner he asked him if he knew why he was being arrested and what the charge was and Turner replied, "Yes, sir, for the murdering of those two men in the broom factory."

The city hall in Philadelphia in those days was a combination of many things. It housed all of the city and county courts, the city and county government offices, it was the central police station and it was also the jail. It was there that all three men were placed for a period of time while they were questioned.

The first day Turner got there he was put into a private cell and then taken out by detectives to one of their offices in the city hall where they talked to him for three hours. He denied any connection with the broom factory murders. When he was put back in his cell that night he pushed a bucket against the wall and grabbed the bars that ran along the open ceiling. In a barely audible voice, he told Jasper Johnson, whom he had seen a few cells down, to "stand tight and not to talk." What Jasper heard, so did a guard who was policing the cells. Later that night Turner was transferred to the station house at 15th and Snyder and in the morning he was taken back to city hall for more questioning when he promised he would not try to influence other prisoners. On June 4, 1946, he was taken from his cell and again questioned by two officers. Nothing. He was innocent, he said. He didn't know a thing about Lofton and Johnson; he only knew them casually. The next day the questioning

32

was resumed by different detectives but there was no change in Turner's attitude.

Then on the evening of June 6, detectives, Thompson and O'Mahoney, hid in the cell next to one where all three suspects had been placed. After a while they heard Johnson say, Hey, Tree, why the detectives asking all them questions?" There was some low conversation about the broom factory and then Turner said, "I had to hit the second fellow awfully hard, twice, and the blood came out of his ears."

Late the next day, while two detectives were talking to Turner in his cell he told them, "I want to tell the truth." One of the detectives told him that he better realize that if he did tell them anything his statements would be used against him. He nodded and then said, "I killed those guys in the factory." Now the police had the corroboration they needed to go along with Lofton's testimony.

While detectives were talking to Turner, others were talking to Johnson and Lofton, getting nowhere until someone pointed out to Johnson that he had been cheated on the loot, that Turner got the biggest share even though Johnson was the guy who first spotted the place and conceived the whole thing. Johnson did not like that, and after satisfying himself that he had been gypped, he confessed fully, not only to his participation in the murders but to Turner's and Lofton's also. Now all three had confessed.

At 9 a.m., June 8, detectives began taking Johnson's statement, talking, typing, talking, typing, making corrections, writing. When they were finished, all three men - Turner, Johnson, and Lofton - were brought into an office in the city hall and each of their typewritten statements was read to all three of them. Since none had anything to add to the way the confessions were written, each signed his own statement. Then, to make sure they were also acknowledging that what the other two said was correct, they were asked to sign the statements of the other two and they did, signing each page of each other's statement.

Turner's statement was glib and short. He said he told Johnson and Lofton, "We have a job to do, and they went with me...when we passed in the second door we met the man and I hit the man with a piece of iron which I had wrapped up in a piece of newspaper. Q. When you say you looked the place over, the broom factory...what did you have in mind? A. I figured it was quiet around there and I figured it was easy money to rob."

Johnson backed him up, "We were met by the smallest fellow, a middle-aged man. Treetop slugged him on the side of the head. The fellow was on the floor scuffling, trying to get up. I runs in his pocket pulls out a wallet out of the hip pocket....I looks around to see Treetop and the other man. He was on the floor and Tree was over him. He had done slugged him."

Lofton, who was the lookout, heard "Treetop" say, as he and "Playboy" were leaving the factory, "One of them wasn't no trouble at all but one of the sons of bitches I had to give a hell of a blow to."

After the statements were signed, the police asked all three if they would go back to the scene and demonstrate exactly what they had done. Johnson and Lofton said they didn't care. Turner went, but didn't say a word.

At the broom factory, Lofton showed the police where they were standing across the street waiting for the place to close and where he stood when the other two went in. Johnson took them into the factory and pointed out where they met the first man and how Turner hit him and then hurried to the back of the store to hit the other one. Turner just stood around at the scene and said nothing, not even a nod to anything Lofton or Johnson said.

When they finished, they were taken back to their cells at the city hall. The police were now ready to take their case to court. They readied the paper work and then, after a short consultation with the district attorney's office, it was decided that the three would appear before a magistrate right away and have the preliminary hearing in a few days.

Johnson was impatient, he wanted to get it over with and get on his way. The officers told all three that after they had signed the statements a formal complaint would be typed and filed and then they would be taken before a judge, a city magistrate, whose job was to tell them officially what they were charged with and to inform them they had a right to a preliminary hearing to see if the Commonwealth had enough evidence to take them to trial. Within an hour, all three were standing before a magistrate. The formal charge was read to them and then it was explained that each would have a preliminary hearing in a couple of days. No one expected the hearing to take very long. They had each confessed, not only once but actually two or three times; once all alone, once each time they signed each other's statement, and then again when two of them reenacted the crime while Turner stood by and watched.

Five days later the preliminary hearing began. The detectives testified as to what they saw at the murder scene, the treatment of the defendants and their subsequent confessions. They testified that the confessions were not coerced and they were offered into evidence. The judge gave each of the defendants time to ask questions about the officers' testimony' but they declined the opportunity and the confessions were admitted. With that, the state closed its case; there was really nothing more to say or to show, the dead bodies had been identified and the confessions connected each defendant directly to the crime.

The judge explained to the defendants that they could now make a statement if they wanted to but that they did not have to. Lofton said that he wanted to tell about it, the way it happened, and he did tell his story, just like he told it in the written confession, implicating himself, Johnson and Turner in a premeditated murder and robbery. When he finished, Johnson spoke up and told his story - the same thing he said in his confession. Turner, however, didn't say much. It was all in his statement, he said, he didn't need to give the Commonwealth any more.

In an hour and a half it was all over. The defendants were returned to the station where they were questioned further about the Ace Broom case and others. More official papers were drawn up – "Murder in The First Degree," but only for the death of Endres. The prosecution decided to hold the other murder charge (Simmons) back in case it was needed later. Within a matter of days the grand jury returned three true bills charging all three with murder and the cases were set for trial in the Court of Quarter Sessions.

Shortly after that, Lofton pleaded guilty to first degree murder. Although nothing was said in court at the time he entered the plea, it was obvious to those who understood the system that the plea was part of a bargain struck with the Commonwealth to help it convict the other two. Later, Lofton would receive a life sentence and testify against Turner.

Johnson's trial was severed from Turner's and lasted eight days. He was convicted of murder in the first degree and the jury set the penalty at death. Death in Pennsylvania at the time meant the electric chair.

At his own trial, Turner denied the truth of his confessions. He maintained to the court and to the jury that the statements had been extracted from him by pressure, by sweating, and prolonged questioning and that if it had not been for those things he would not have confessed.

At the end of the testimony the court told the jury that no confession could be admitted into evidence and considered by the

35

jury until the jury had satisfied itself beyond a reasonable doubt that the confession was given of the defendant's own free will without fear or coercion.

The jury did not believe Turner; they accepted his confession, convicted him of first degree murder and set his penalty at death.

Turner filed a motion for a new trial. His main argument was that his confession had been induced by fear and coercion and should not have been considered by the jury. The trial judge disagreed. It was obvious, he said, that Turner was not a poor negro with a low intellect. From watching him throughout the trial, the judge said, Turner appeared smart and clever and not really annoyed or controlled by other minds. His confession was obviously not concocted by others and it was entirely consistent with his guilt and his actions, as well as that of his confederates. In addition, the judge added, Turner's confession flatly stated that he was telling his story in his own words and that no one coerced him or physically abused him. With that, the judge denied Turner's motion.

Turner's lawyer, Edwin P. Rome, then started on the journey that now seems incredible - he filed the first of five appeals. As he had in the trial court, Mr. Rome argued to the Pennsylvania Supreme Court that Turner's confessions had been taken from him (there was more than one remember, and all had been introduced against him at his trial) involuntarily, wrung from him by fear, physical abuse and offensive interrogation. As make-weight, he contended that the confessions were completely false and also that their taking was unfair because Turner did not have an attorney with him at the time and he was not taken before a magistrate to be formally told of his rights with any kind of dispatch.

The Pennsylvania Supreme Court disagreed with Mr. Rome. There was no precedent in Pennsylvania, they pointed out in a lengthy opinion, that required suspects to have lawyers present during the giving of confessions. They also found that the interrogation had not been offensive and that, contrary to Turner's contentions, there had been no physical abuse.

As to the truth of the confessions, they noted the trial judge's comment from the record:

"[T]he defendant is not a poor negro of a low degree of intelligence. From an observation of him and listening to his testimony, it is apparent that he is a smart, clever individual. It is

36

apparent that his confession was not concocted by others, and it is clear that it is not a fabrication created by another mind or minds. The statement as given by the defendant is logical and consistent with his guilt and that of his confederates. It shows that the defendant had this broom factory under observation two days before the murders and that his confederates went to the factory on that Saturday afternoon after the close of the business day, for the purpose of robbery....The confession of the defendant and the confessions of his confederates stated what each gave to the other in the way of cash after they had fled from the scene of their crimes. The confession of the defendant shows that in going out Callowill Street, he threw the sash weight away; that the three confederates then went to saloons where they had some drinks, and that they then parted, promising each other that they would say nothing about the crime. A reading of the confession shows that the defendant was asked whether he had been threatened or harmed and whether he had been promised anything, and it also contains the caution that anything he might say might be used against him. The defendant was asked if he knew, when he was arrested, what the charge was and he said, 'yes, sir, for the murdering of those two men in the broom factory.' "

The Supreme Court opinion ended on an optimistic note expressing confidence that if the case ever reached the United States Supreme Court that august body would defer to its long-standing rule of paying respect and giving great weight to a state court's interpretation of its own constitution and uphold the conviction.

Mr. Turner, concluded a unanimous Court, would simply have to be returned to prison where his sentence of death would be carried out.

From there, Mr. Rome took the case to the United States Supreme Court and fifteen months later argued the same contentions in that Court. There it was obvious that the Pennsylvania Supreme Court's trust had been misplaced. The United States Supreme Court reversed Turner's conviction and ordered a new trial.

Noting that Turner had been arrested "on suspicion," later booked "for questioning," had been denied permission to see friends, did not have an attorney, was not warned of his right to remain silent until he made an incriminating statement, was told by the police that other suspects had "opened up" on him when that was not true, was interrogated at length intermittently by a number of detectives, and the district attorney had delayed having the preliminary hearing for 5 days, the United States Supreme Court, in a short 11 paragraph opinion written by Mr. Justice Frankfurter, decided that it simply couldn't let Mr. Turner's confessions be used against him. The only proper conclusion, they said, was that the confessions had been taken from him in violation of his rights under the Fourteenth Amendment to the United States Constitution. Mr. Justice Douglas filed a concurring opinion in which he agreed with the result and noted that "the reason petitioner was not brought before a magistrate was because he had not given the answers which the police wanted and which they believed he could give." The entire matter, he said, was a "vivid illustration of the use of illegal detentions to exact confessions." Three justices, who did not write an opinion, said that they thought the conviction and sentence should be affirmed.

Then the Court threw in a gratuity that proved to be immensely valuable to Turner later on. Barely taking its breath after the eight rapid-fire paragraphs it took to dispose of Turner's confessions, the Court turned to a subject that up to this point in the case had been in the background - the confessions of Johnson and Lofton that Turner had also signed, making them his. These two confessions had also been introduced against Turner at the trial and since the Court anticipated the state might use them again at the new trial they concluded "these confessions call for notice." Clearly, said the Court, these confessions constitutionally fared no better than the one Turner gave in his own hand. The Court conjectured that even though these confessions would not be constitutionally admissible against Turner as his own statement there just might be some quaint Pennsylvania evidentiary rule that would allow them to be introduced as statements of co-principals and thus indirectly harmful to Turner. If that were to happen, the Court indicated, there might once again be constitutional trouble. And that was the end of the discussion - a conjecture, a surmise, a knowing glance.

The prosecution was now left without Turner's direct confessions and it was fairly obvious that if they used the indirect ones they were headed for the same kind of constitutional trouble. The alternative, however, was equally bleak - no confession at all.

Obviously, the Commonwealth had to reassess its case against Turner. Without the confessions was there sufficient evidence left to take the case to trial and if there was, was there a likelihood of a jury convicting? The first decision was fairly easy to make - there was enough evidence to retry Turner. The best piece of evidence against Turner was Lofton, the accomplice. He had participated in the planning of the robbery, he had participated in the robbery itself as a lookout and then he shared in the stolen money when it was finished. His testimony alone was enough to establish a prima facie case. But there were two problems with his testimony. First, he had not been inside the factory when the killings were committed. All he could testify to was that a robbery had been planned, and it was reasonable to conclude that the two who were going into the factory were going to do anything necessary to get the money, including killing, and that the killings were accomplished while Turner and Johnson were in there. Since Lofton did not see the killings; he could only testify to circumstances that indicated (rather forcefully) that Turner and Johnson had killed. This left the jury open to consider other possibilities; that Johnson had done the killings, that Turner had not helped in the killings, and that he had no idea that there would be killings. These were remote possibilities for they seemed unreasonable inferences but they were nevertheless possibilities and things which, if inferred, could allow a jury to reduce the degree of guilt or even acquit. The fact that such inferences could not be drawn legally and would not even be the subject of an instruction to the jury by the court was really immaterial to the Commonwealth in its reassessment of the case. The prosecutors knew that such inferences are drawn by juries regardless of what the law is and they knew that verdicts are sometimes based on such inferences. This is sometimes called "jury law" and regardless of its propriety, it must be considered.

The second problem with Lofton's testimony, of course, was that it was the word of an accomplice, which had to be corroborated with other, additional evidence linking Turner to the murders. At the first trial that was not a problem, Turner's various statements tied him to the murders. But now, the most forceful statements, his confessions, could not be used to establish corroboration. The Commonwealth also could not use the reenactments of the crime performed by Lofton and Johnson in Turner's presence even though Turner was there and watched without protest, because Turner had said nothing, refused to participate, and in no obvious way acquiesced in the reenactments. Legally that does not add up to a confession and even if it did, in all likelihood it would be prohibited by the United States Supreme Court. Thus, the reenactments were out also. The corroboration would have to be found elsewhere - another witness, another participant, another piece of evidence.

One thing came to mind - the statements made by Turner at the preliminary hearing. They implicated him directly in the crime and they backed up what Lofton had to say. Even though they had been introduced as evidence at the first trial not much had been made of them at that time for they were not that important compared to Turner's confessions to the police. The confessions were full and complete; the statements made at the preliminary hearing were not. They admitted only certain incriminating facts and did not purport to tell a full, fluid story. Their purpose when made was to give the magistrate only enough facts for him to determine whether the three should remain in jail and wait for trial. Very seldom at that stage does the prosecution attempt to present a full story of the crime and frequently only the important highlights are told. The nuances are usually left for the trial. Still, the preliminary hearing statements made by Turner were damaging admissions, they did corroborate parts of Lofton's testimony and they were not infected with the unconstitutionality the Supreme Court spied in the confessions. The Commonwealth reasoned that the statements at the preliminary hearing were a break in the chain of oppressive circumstances that led to the now involuntary confessions; they were not extracted by the police, they were given to a magistrate at a lawfully recognized hearing (one actually required by law) and they were not given in the coercive atmosphere of the station house but in a courtroom, though a minor one capable of handling only the most preliminary matters in felony prosecutions.

With these things determined, the Commonwealth built its second prosecution around Lofton and the preliminary hearing admissions of Turner. The jury convicted Turner and again imposed a death sentence. After post-verdict motions, the verdict was upheld by the trial court and the case was appealed to the Pennsylvania Supreme Court.

As had been expected, Mr. Rome attacked the Commonwealth's corroboration evidence directly, arguing that the preliminary hearing statements were no different from the confessions to the police which previously had been ruled invalid. The court agreed, seeing little difference between the confessions and the admissions at the hearing. First, they said, the courtroom where the preliminary hearing was held was just another room in the same city hall where the interrogations had taken place. Then, they continued: "The only persons present at this hearing were the same police officers who had engaged in the questioning, the magistrate and an assistant district attorney. After one of the police officers testified, the three defendants were sworn and Johnson testified in detail as to how the crime was committed and of the participation of each of the three men. Lofton and Turner then without the same detail affirmed Johnson's account of the commission of the crime. Although the magistrate thereupon held the defendants 'without bail for the court,' they were not committed to the county prison but turned over to the same police officers and detained in the latter's custody."

After reviewing the United States Supreme Court opinion, the court summarized: "Turner's signed written confession has been deemed the result of inherent coercion. Certainly statements or admissions which he made at the preliminary hearing held during the coercive period and prior to his execution of the condemned confessions must be considered tainted by the same infirmity. It is evident that the United States Supreme Court did not regard the interlude of the preliminary hearing as having purged the coercion. We are constrained to hold, therefore, that the testimony taken at the magistrate's hearing was inadmissible as evidence against Turner as was his confession."

Then, as a parting thrust, the Pennsylvania Supreme Court cautioned the trial court to be more careful in its attitude toward the accomplice, Lofton, at the retrial. The testimony of accomplices, the Court noted, is to be carefully scrutinized, not only because of any interest an accomplice might have in the outcome of the case but also because such testimony comes from a corrupt source - a confessed criminal. At the second trial, Mr. Rome had requested the trial court to charge the jury they were to view the accomplice's testimony with great caution and reluctance. Erroneously, the trial court told Mr. Rome that the law did not require the jury to view an accomplice with such a jaundiced eye and therefore the trial court refused to instruct them in that manner. The Pennsylvania Supreme Court cautioned that Mr. Rome had correctly stated the law and that any similar requests in the future were to be given. In the future, then, Lofton's testimony must be taken with a grain of salt and the jury must be handed that salt by the trial court. With little else left to do, the conviction was reversed. Treetop Turner would now stand trial for a third time.

One month later the third trial was held. This time the Commonwealth's case rested primarily upon Lofton's testimony.

Instead of the confessions, the reenactments and the preliminary hearing statements as corroboration, the Commonwealth had to reach back for a bit of evidence that was of minor significance at the second trial and had not even been used at the first trial - eavesdropping of Turner by detectives Thompson and O'Mahoney. Shortly after their arrest, Turner and his two cohorts had been placed together in a cell. During an interlude in their interrogation the two detectives hid in an adjoining cell and overheard Turner tell the others that he had a tough time with the second man. As O'Mahoney related the conversation at the third trial:

"The voice I heard sounded like Jasper Johnson's voice. He said, 'Hey, Tree, why are the detectives asking all them questions?' There was a reference made to something about a broom factory. The answer came back 'I had to hit the second fellow -.' "

"Q. Who said that?"

"A. This defendant, Aaron Turner."

"Q. What did he say?"

"A. He said, 'I had to hit the second fellow awfully hard twice and the blood came out of his ears.' "

Later, much would be made of the fact that this very damaging testimony had not been used at the first trial. Although the record of that trial does not reveal why it was not used there are rather obvious and reasonable explanations. First, it was eavesdropping evidence, secrets gained by stealth. There is nothing illegal about this type of eavesdropping; it is not equated with wiretapping or mechanical bugging. But it is deceit and even when done for the public safety it does not ordinarily sit well with juries. Jurors do not relish the thought of convicting someone based upon something he said in private to a friend intending that that friend alone hear it. Anyone, even a policeman, who secretly positions himself so that he can intrude on this privacy has dealt with the individual unfairly. The second reason is that whatever is heard by eavesdropping is sometimes suspect simply because of the way in which it was heard. Ordinarily the eavesdropper is out of sight, hidden and not usually in a position where he can hear things clearly or accurately determine who was talking. Because of this, cross-examination on occasion renders eavesdropping testimony innocuous, or worse, suspect.

Nevertheless, eavesdropping testimony sometimes may be necessary - it was at "Treetop" Turner's third trial because there was nothing else. Even with it, the Commonwealth's case was not that strong for it gave the jurors too many pegs to hang a reasonable doubt on. Put yourself in the place of a juror at that third trial. First, there were the usual witnesses to establish that a murder had been committed, the time, the place, method, instrument used, etc. - all the essential facts showing a *corpus delicti* and setting the stage for the evidence that links the defendant to the act. Next there was Lofton, a confessed murder-robbery participant, an accomplice whose testimony the judge warned the jury must be viewed with caution because he was a confessed criminal and received a lighter sentence in exchange for his testimony against Turner.

Lofton told the jury he didn't see the killings, but he wanted the jury to believe that he knew who had done them – Turner and Johnson. But did they both kill? Or did only one kill? And if it was only one, which one was it? Johnson was never seen at and was not heard from at Turner's trial (because of the 5th Amendment, he could not be called as a witness at any of Turner's trials because he was fighting for his own life in another courtroom on the same charges). Thus, other than Lofton's tainted testimony, the only evidence linking Turner to the crime was the eavesdropping testimony of the two detectives. Once that was presented the Commonwealth rested its case. In many ways, the case, although it bore the label Commonwealth v. Turner, bore only a fleeting resemblance to the original, actual case.

Yet for a third time, "Treetop" Turner was convicted of first-degree murder and sentenced to death. In May of 1952 the conviction reached the Pennsylvania Supreme Court and it went no further. Once again Mr. Rome attacked one of Turner's utterances - now, of course, the only one left, the one overheard by the officers. Rome's argument, interestingly enough, was based upon fairly recent case law concerning utterances from the United States Supreme Court - Turner v. Pennsylvania. Things had now come full circle; Turner was citing himself as reason for his own reversal.

Essentially, Mr. Rome was arguing that the coercion noted by the United States Supreme Court three years earlier was so pervasive that it infected all of Turner's statements from the time of his arrest through the preliminary hearing and even after. But the Pennsylvania Supreme Court disagreed, noting a basic distinction between the confessions and statements already condemned and the one overheard and presented at the third trial. The condemned statements, they said, were the direct result of coercive police tactics; the overheard statement was not coerced directly and was not an indirect outgrowth of that coercion.

43

But there was more to the opinion. At the third trial, Mr. Rome asked the trial judge at the very beginning to instruct all witnesses that they were not to be in the courtroom when someone else was testifying and they were not to talk to each other or anyone about their testimony except the lawyers. In particular, Mr. Rome wanted the eavesdropping detectives Thompson and O'Mahoney kept from hearing each other's testimony. The object, of course, was to have the testimony of each uninfluenced by the other's testimony. As Mr. Rome put it: "Detectives Thompson and O'Mahoney testified fully in the first trial, because they were the police officers that investigated and tracked it down. In the second trial they testified again, and for the first time testified to having overheard conversations in the cell room that went to the heart of the case. They admitted they had not spoken of that before....It would give us opportunity to cross-examine each witness in turn regarding the detail of that, and if the second man is in the Court I submit the defendant has not adequate opportunity to cross-examine under the circumstances."

Recognizing that Pennsylvania law permitted this type of sequestration but only in extraordinary circumstances, the trial judge felt that nothing extraordinary had been shown and he denied the defense request to keep the witnesses out of the courtroom and to prohibit them from talking to other witnesses. But the Pennsylvania Supreme Court disagreed. "We can conceive of no case more appropriate or compelling," said the Court, "for the sequestration of witnesses than that under the circumstances of this case." So, the trial judge was correct on the law but wrong in its application - this was an extraordinary case and the defense request should have been granted. Because it was not, the third conviction was reversed and a new trial, the fourth, was ordered. For future reference it is interesting to note that in winding down this opinion, the Court was careful to point out that they had not formed any opinions about the truthfulness of the officers' testimony. Those opinions, they said, were properly left to the jury's discretion, which is where they should be left. Jurors see and hear the witnesses. A knowing look, a glance, a sign, a flash of excitement - these things often show much more about the telling of a lie than black words on a white page. That is why appellate courts leave such decisions to juries. Almost always, that is. We shall hear more of this later.

The fourth trial. Here a surprise awaited the prosecution - Lofton refused to testify. When he took the stand he answered a few preliminary questions and then simply stopped.

"Q. You testified against Treetop Turner three times, didn't you?"

"A. (No Answer.)"

"Q. And the testimony that you gave against him was the testimony that I said here today, isn't that right? Were you telling the truth or is this man innocent and you were lying, and getting him into the jail and to the death house?"

"A. Take it any way you wish. I told you I am not answering any more questions."

"Q. Was it the truth? Is Treetop Turner innocent? You said he was guilty. This man was sentenced to the electric chair three times on your testimony."

"A. (No Answer.)."

Then Lofton blurted out: "Just a minute, Chief. When you was up (at the Eastern State Penitentiary) last week I told you I had been tried and convicted and I preferred to have no more to say or do with the case. I am doing my time; I am doing life. There is nothing else I can say in no way, shape or form."

Lofton was obviously sick and tired of a system that couldn't get on with its business, a system that tolerated interminable delays and couldn't seem to get down to the real issue - guilt or innocence. Here it was eight years after the murders, three juries and three death penalties later and the system still could not make up its mind about "Treetop" Turner. Undoubtedly it must have occurred to Lofton that this system was its own worst enemy and he wasn't going to give it any more help.

Fortunately for the Commonwealth, there was a transcript of Lofton's testimony. The district attorney sought and received permission to read that former testimony to the jury and for the fourth time a jury convicted Turner of first-degree murder and set the penalty at death. And the penalty was especially interesting because the Commonwealth had not asked the jury to return a death sentence.

Again the defense appealed, relying in the main on the reading of Lofton's prior testimony. For a time at least, the point got nowhere; such a reading, as noted by the trial court at the time, was specifically provided for in the Pennsylvania Code. But there was something else amiss - the prosecutor's comment when questioning Lofton that Turner had been sentenced to the electric chair on three prior occasions. This remark could not even muster a low passing grade at the appellate division of the trial court, the Quarter Session Court of Philadelphia County, convened to pass upon post-trial motions. There, on a motion for new trial the fourth conviction and fourth death penalty were overturned and Turner was given a new trial. The district attorney's remarks, said the court, "were so prejudicial to defendant's right to a fair trial that the error could not be cured by the charge of the trial judge. We do not doubt that the remarks were made unintentionally by the district attorney during the heat of the trial but this fact does not purge the statement of its prejudicial taint. Once the statement was made, the court had no device at its disposal to render the proceedings free from prejudice so as to satisfy the requirements of due process. In view of this we have no alternative but to award defendant Aaron Turner a new trial."

The fifth trial. This would be the last and there were more problems. Before the argument on the motion for the new trial after conviction number four, Lofton had called his attorney and told him he wanted to see him at the prison. When he did, Lofton recanted all of his prior testimony and signed a notarized statement saying he knew nothing of Turner's involvement in the murder. The statement was filed with the appeals court as another ground for overturning the fourth conviction - the main witness against Turner now stated that his testimony was perjured. But the opinion of the appeals court never reached that point.

In preparing for the fifth trial, the district attorney went to talk with Lofton about his recanting affidavit that he knew nothing of Turner's involvement. He would not budge, he said, everything he had testified to against Turner was false and if called to the stand at the fifth trial he would say Turner had nothing to do with the killings. Nevertheless, the prosecutor had to put Lofton on the stand. It is not uncommon for accomplices who have pleaded guilty and are serving their sentences to say that the story they told years ago was a lie, that the alleged accomplice actually had nothing to do with the crime. One justice of the Pennsylvania Supreme Court's said of Lofton's recantation, "This is merely in accord with the code of the underworld not to 'rat' on each other." But it is also not uncommon for accomplices who recant to cave in and go back to their original story when put on the stand and sworn in. In many cases, a district attorney has to call the accomplice's bluff because he doesn't know what story the accomplice will tell until he puts him on the stand and asks the questions. In this case there was nothing else the Commonwealth had - without Lofton's story there was no case against Turner. If Lofton refused to testify again, the district attorney planned to ask the trial court to declare Lofton unavailable as a witness and allow him to read Lofton's previous testimony just as the trial judge had done at the fourth trial. So the Commonwealth called Lofton at the fifth trial and he carried out his threat - at first he refused to testify, in fact he refused to speak at all. For refusing, he was held in contempt by the trial court and time was added to his sentence. But that had little effect; he was serving a life sentence and he had already served 10 years. The district attorney turned back to Lofton and tried again. Lofton told the judge that the only thing he was willing to do was to testify in accordance with his affidavit of recantation that Turner had nothing to do with the killings. The district attorney then asked the court to declare Lofton an unavailable witness and allow his prior testimony implicating Turner to be read to the jury. But the trial judge refused. This witness was not unavailable, he said, he was in the courtroom, he was on the witness stand, and he was not refusing to testify - he was simply saying that he would no longer testify as he had before. "This man has been called as a witness. He says that this paper (the recanting affidavit) is the truth and he says he wants to tell the truth. In other words, he wants to testify to those facts." The district attorney tried another tack. Holding the recanting affidavit in his hand, he asked:

"Q. You signed it and you swore it was the truth; is that right?

"A. I did.

"Q. And you still maintain that that is the truth; is that right?

"A. I do.

"Q. Now I will read you what you said in that Affidavit.

'I, Clarence Lofton, made the following statement freely and voluntarily without any threats or promises made to me.

'Although I have testified against Aaron Turner and Jasper Johnson and have said that they took part with me in the robbery of the Ace Broom Factory at 355 North Second Street, Philadelphia, Pennsylvania, which led to the killing of two men named Charles Simmons and Frank Endres, everything I have ever said which connects these two men in any way with that crime is untrue. So far as I know, neither Jasper Johnson nor Aaron Turner had anything to do

47

with that crime. Moreover, even though I pleaded guilty to participating in that crime, I never had anything to do with it either.'

"Q. Now, do you say that is true?"

"A. I do."

Then the district attorney turned to the trial judge and asked him to declare Lofton a hostile witness and allow the district attorney to cross-examine him. In most states when one side places a witness on the stand and then discovers he is a hostile witness, which usually means he has said or is prepared to say things helpful to the other side, the side who placed him on the stand will ask the judge to declare the witness hostile to the party who called him and allow the questioner to attack him (cross examine him). Ordinarily when a party puts a witness on the stand he vouches for his credibility and he cannot attack him. If he is declared hostile, however, an attack is proper. Lofton was hostile and the district attorney wanted to attack him. The court realized what was going on and he knew that under Pennsylvania's rules of procedure even though Lofton was hostile the district attorney could not get the right to cross examine unless he also claimed that he was surprised at Lofton's hostility. In theory at least, if a prosecutor knows before he puts a witness on the stand that that witness will not testify the way the prosecutor expects him to, he cannot place that witness on the stand and then attack him by showing prior statements he made. He may attack the witness only when he places him on the stand and is genuinely surprised at the turn of events. Here the court broached the issue:

"The Court desires to ask you one question, Mr. Panati (the district attorney). Do I understand you are surprised at the testimony?

"Mr. Panati: That is precisely the Commonwealth's position.

"The Court: And you plead surprise?

"Mr. Panati: I do, sir

"The Court: The objection (Turner's objection to Lofton's being cross examined) is overruled. Exception noted for the defendant."

And with that, the district attorney proceeded with leading questions to Lofton to bring out all of his prior testimony implicating Turner. This plus the eavesdropping testimony of Thompson and O'Mahoney was enough for the fifth jury to convict Turner again of first degree murder but this time they set the sentence at life imprisonment. No one knows why; they simply did it.

Once again Mr. Rome prepared his appeal He concentrated on the reading of Lofton's prior testimony and the eavesdropping conversation picked up by the two detectives. He was well aware that the removal of either would mean the end of the case.

It was in the summer of 1957 that Mr. Rome took his case before the Pennsylvania Supreme Court and there it took a final, freakish twist. The conviction was reversed and the case sent back to the trial court with an admonition that if the state could not produce more evidence than it had at the fourth trial Turner must be released. The reversal itself was not so bad, that had happened before. And even the admonition that Turner had to be released if more evidence was not produced was not so shocking, that had to be expected sooner or later as the courts kept knocking off bits of evidence.

What was so shocking and inexplicable was the tone of the opinion of the Pennsylvania Supreme Court. It was almost as though the Court was speaking of another case. The district attorney was severely chastised for his persistent efforts to get Lofton's prior testimony into evidence and before the jury. The trial judge was taken to task for suggesting an avenue for the prosecutor to follow in his efforts to get the evidence in ("And you plead surprise?") and the credibility of Detectives Thompson and O'Mahoney was completely destroyed. The Court figuratively sneered at the officers for not bringing up the eavesdropping testimony at the first trial, belittled the fact that they could remember such a conversation after five years without having taken notes at the time, and related an incident at the fifth trial which at least to a majority of the Pennsylvania Supreme Court insured their lack of credibility and rendered their testimony "so lacking in probative value as to be incapable of supporting a verdict which would deprive the defendant of either his life or liberty."

The incident was trivial. It concerned the trial court's order sequestering the witnesses. Before the testimony began, the court announced "We will direct that all witnesses be segregated and that they be kept out of the courtroom except when testifying. And we also instruct all witnesses that they are not to discuss this case among themselves or with any other witness at any time during the continuance of this trial...If there is any witness who didn't understand the court's instruction, please let us know now." No responses. "All right. All you witnesses remove yourselves from the court room and don't come back until you are called." And the trial began. Three witnesses testified for the state and then the court broke for lunch. Mr. Rome went to a restaurant a block from the city hall. When he entered he saw Detectives O'Mahoney and Thompson at a table "located in the back of the restaurant behind a large column or pillar." He walked over to them. As he approached, Thompson faced him and O'Mahoney's back was to him. When he reached their table, he placed his hand on O'Mahoney's shoulder "to make certain that he, too, knew of counsel's presence." O'Mahoney turned around and held a paper napkin to his face as if to disguise himself. Later, O'Mahoney would explain to the trial court that he was merely clowning. But the Pennsylvania Supreme Court didn't see it that way. To them, O'Mahoney's "pantomime was the instinctive reaction of a guilty conscience." It mattered little to the Court that both detectives testified at the time of the incident that they had not discussed the case during that luncheon break. When the Court finished with the two, their testimony was "inherently so unreliable as not to justify a finding beyond a reasonable doubt that the conversation (Turner's eavesdropping conversation) did actually occur as O'Mahoney and Thompson have testified." That, of course, finished that bit of evidence; it could not in good conscience ever be used again. This is the same testimony, you may remember, that the same court refused to form opinions about after the third trial. A unanimous court in that prior opinion stated that such opinions were properly left to the jury.

Two concurring justices scorned the majority for reversing themselves. "[H]ow is it possible," they said, "for the majority to justify its present statements or position!...From time immemorial it has been the province of the jury to pass upon the credibility of witnesses....Four times the juries and the trial judges believed these details. Yet today the majority of this Court who of course did not see the witnesses (a) not only disagree with the juries and with the trial courts on their credibility, but (b) arrogate to themselves the power to disbelieve the clear, positive, and in all material respects consistent testimony of witnesses they did not see and to obliterate their testimony which they admit was admissible." As to Lofton and his credibility and the district attorney's efforts to bring out his prior testimony, the dissenters said "Lofton, 10 years after pleading guilty to these murders and after all these years in jail, now swears that he and Turner and Johnson never committed or had anything to do with these murders. How gullible can we be?"

But the majority of the Court was not through. Next, they attacked the eavesdropped conversation itself. First they pooh-poohed eavesdropping testimony as "the weakest and most suspicious kind of evidence" and then decided that what the detectives thought they may have heard was not what it seemed to be. No reasonable juror could rationally conclude, they said, that "that broom place" in the conversation meant the Ace Broom Factory and that the "second man" referred to by Turner was one of the two men found dead in the Ace Broom Factory. At this, the concurring justices lashed out again. This was the same evidence, they reminded the others, that a unanimous court held constitutional and properly admissible at the third trial and had characterized in these words – "in the instant case there can be no misinterpretation of the words purportedly used by Turner...,"exactly contrary to what the majority opinion now asserted.

Then, incredibly, the majority of the court, trying to avoid even suggesting Turner's guilt, referred to that possibility only as an "idea" and concluded that "Were it not for the idea of defendant's guilt, which the written confessions in this case originally created, but which those confessions (since completely invalidated) are no longer capable of establishing, it is inconceivable that the conversation between Johnson and Turner, which the detectives claim to have overheard, would ever have been deemed by anyone as constituting a conclusive admission by the defendant of his guilt of the murder which, except for the invalid confessions, he has at all times denied and which the Commonwealth, to date, has failed to prove by legally competent evidence."

A second concurring opinion by Justice Michael Musmanno agreeing with the majority, added an Alice In Wonderland finish. He saw the whole affair as a triumph for the American system of democracy. "And now that an eleven-year continuous endeavor for justice has apparently reached the only conclusion it should have reached, I cannot help but express a renewed and continuing admiration for lawyers who, despite rebuffs and seeming failure, carry on, in the tribunals set up by the genius and the fairness of the American people, in the search for the priceless jewel of truth..." "The ascertainment of the exact truth," he called it; the vindication of "an innocent man (who) might probably have gone to an undeserved death."

Innocent man? Sixty jurors from five different juries had found him guilty. Five judges agreed and four death penalties had been levied upon him.

Two weeks after the opinion, the First Assistant District Attorney went before the trial judge in Philadelphia.

"After the fifth appeal," he told the court, "the State Supreme Court made an order ordering a new trial and adding that a nol pros (technically 'nolle prosequi,' a formal declaration by the prosecutor that he will no longer pursue the case) be entered on the indictment if there were not more evidence. Following the reading of that order, I discussed the matter with Assistant District Attorney Thomas M. Reed, who helped prepare this case for trial on several occasions and argued it last before the State Supreme Court. It is our belief that there is no other evidence than was presented at the fifth trial. Therefore, the district attorney's office moves for the nol pros of all bills (charges) as to Aaron Turner."

The judge, who had been the trial judge at the third trial, said, "in view of what you have said and my own knowledge of this case, the court agrees to nol pros all bills. I didn't think there was any more evidence. I was led to expect this. The prisoner is discharged."

With that, Treetop Turner was released from jail forever. It was October, 1957. His guilt had been proved to five different juries on five different occasions and yet he stands convicted of nothing today and the system pats itself on the back for a job well done by pretending he is innocent.

"When I use a word it means just what I choose it to mean - neither more nor less," said Humpty Dumpty.

Hocus-pocus.

The End

Sources and attributions:

The court opinions can be found in Commonwealth v. Turner at: 358 Pa. 350, 58 A.2d 61 (1948): 338 U.S. 62, 69 S.Ct. 1352, 93 L.Ed.1810 (1949): 367 Pa. 403, 80 A.2d 708 (1951): 371 Pa. 417, 88 A.2d 915 (1952): 1 D. & C.2d 11 (1953) (1955 WL 5027 (Pa.O. & T): 389 Pa. 239, 133 A.2d 187 (1957).

A Most Curious Murder Case

The Arizona State Prison's web site has an entry for every inmate put to death there. For No. 5400, Simplicio Torrez, the entry is very short. He was Mexican, a sheepherder educated at a public school. He was 24 when he was sent to prison by Coconino County. He arrived at the prison on 8/8/19. He had no prior record with the prison and his crime was murder in the 1st degree. His sentence was death. That's it. A few inches below is: "Returned to Coconino County Court and resentenced 1/12/1920 to hang 4/16/20. 4/16/20 Hanged at 10:00 a.m."

But there is a lot more to Simplicio's story. If you looked closely at the dates you saw that there was less than five months between his arriving at the prison and being re-sentenced to death. That's a short time for any appeal in a criminal case, but especially in a death penalty case. Simplicio Torrez wanted to appeal his case to the Arizona Supreme Court, but he was never given the chance.

Simplicio Torrez killed Victor Melick, the Marshall of the Town of Williams by shooting him "in cold blood" on Memorial Day 1919. Marshall Melick was about to arrest him for stealing Mrs. Ambrosia Means's "little black" horse, the one she "rode herself."

Mrs. Means apparently was more than just an average citizen. The local newspaper, the Coconino Sun, pointed out more than once that she was the wife "of a hunter, trapper and guide famous all over the West, having piloted hunting parties of America's most prominent citizens, including Theodore Roosevelt and others." She saw Torrez watering her horse at a trough a short distance from her house and yelled to him, "What are you doing with my horse? Take that saddle off. Who bobbed its mane and tail?" Torrez ignored her and went off with the horse.

Someone notified "the authorities" and they went to Torrez's house. His mother said he wasn't home and they left, but then turned around and knocked on the door again. This time Torrez came to the door. They told him why they were there and he agreed to go with them after he got his coat. But he ran through the house and into a shack out back where he lived. When they took him from the shack he had a .32 caliber pistol hidden in his pants. They told him they were going to take him back to the Means home to get things settled, but he didn't want to go, and anyway, he said, a man had given him permission to take the horse. When they got to the "White Garage" the authority offered to go in and use their telephone to call the man who gave him permission to take the horse. But Torrez said don't bother and they walked on.

As they got to the Means house, Marshall Melick met them and told Torrez he was under arrest. Torrez asked "What for? I haven't done anything," and then he turned to Mrs. Means and asked "What's all the fuss about? Why did you have me arrested." She didn't reply and Torrez said "I want to go eat my supper." Then, according to the Sun, Melick "spoke the last words of his life, little thinking that death was less than five minutes off, 'I haven't had my supper yet; and you can wait as well as I can.' " Torrez pulled out his gun and shot Melick three times in the stomach. "Then Victor Melick, man and gentleman, with three bullets in him, any one of which would have caused his death, proved that the West still breeds men who die without a whimper, and, facing death, think only of the job on hand. Without a cry or moan of any kind, still standing, and without saying a word, he drew his gun, fired three times at the dodging figure before him, and slowly sank to the ground. He was dead within about 5 minutes." Torrez ran back to his shack behind his mother's house.

When the authorities took him into custody they found him inside his shack wounded and bleeding and praying not to be shot. Some of the townspeople had already taken shots at him.

The authorities took him to the jail in Williams and when more townspeople gathered they decided, for his safety, they should get him to the jail in Flagstaff. So they thought of a ruse. They backed up a car to the jail door and pretended Torrez was dead. Torrez must have been part of the plan too. When they brought out his body some in the crowd tried to kick him and one was about to shoot him when one of the authorities said "Don't shoot him; he's dead," and he pointed to the nasty bullet wound in Torrez's side. An inquest was held that night and it determined that Melick "came to his death at the hands of Simplicio Torez (sic)."

The Sun concluded its coverage of the events of the day with this odd touch: "His father and brother have visited him and his mother is staying in the cell with him to nurse him. Torez (sic) had a sister in Seligman who committed suicide about a month ago."

Torrez went to trial in Flagstaff eight weeks later before Superior Court Judge J.E. Jones, and Mr. Torrez was represented by Mercer Hemperley of Flagstaff. The defense announced right away that they would not contest the evidence that Torrez killed

54

Marshall Melick; they would prove that Torrez was insane when he shot.

The jury was picked on Tuesday and the attorneys presented their opening statements that night. Mr. Hemperley told the jury that Torrez "had always been a hard-working, peaceful boy until a few years ago, when he got mixed up with a disreputable woman, who taught him to drink raw alcohol and loco weed and helped him run through his savings of $600 in one month." From that time on, he said, "Torez (sic) was changed, got into trouble frequently and had been adjudged insane and sent to an asylum. He is afflicted with homicidal mania. His sister last April went insane and committed suicide, and he has an uncle in the insane asylum." Mr. Harben, the Assistant County Attorney, told the jury "in a few concise, well-chosen words what the state intended to prove."

The state rested its case the next day and Torrez presented his insanity defense. The Sun said that Torrez's insanity plea "was almost still-born, giving only a few convulsive gasps before it was tenderly laid to rest" when the state introduced a certified copy of his discharge from the insane asylum in Phoenix in 1917 declaring him sane. His mother and father testified that "Simplicio had been good until he was twenty years old and bad after that" and his mother said she thought he was insane and should be cared for. Orville Brown, a cowboy, called to the stand to say that Torrez was insane, disappointed the defense by testifying that he thought (Torrez) "was simply a bad Mexican."

The trial ended on Friday, July 18, 1919 and the jury returned its verdict after deliberating just 7 minutes - guilty of murder in the first degree with a sentence of death. The judge set the formal sentencing and entry of judgment for August 4, 1919. The Sun noted: "So far there have been no sensations sprung at the trial of Simplicio Torez (sic), the young Mexican degenerate..." And "with only a few weeks longer to live, Torez (sic) wears the same braggadocio afire as ever. While in jail he bought blankets from an Indian and then did not pay him. Pinned to Torez's (sic) undershirt was a silver-plated star labeled United States Detective, where he got it, is not known. Probably he had lots of fun passing himself off as an officer. "

The next step by Mr. Hemperley was to appeal, to get the case before the Arizona Supreme Court and convince them to reverse the verdict and sentence. But first, certain things had to be done in the trial court. According to the Rules of Procedure, Mr.Torrez had to give Judge Jones the opportunity to correct any grave errors at the trial or permit M. Torrez to present newly discovered evidence by granting him a new trial. If that is denied, the judge has to approve the verdict of the jury with a formal judgment and then a notice of appeal may be filed with Arizona Supreme Court.

Mr. Hemperley filed a motion for a new trial, arguing he now had positive evidence that Mr. Torrez was insane. The evidence was an affidavit of Dawson Henderson, a 21-year old man who had known Torrez for a few years when he employed him in "sheep camps." The affidavit said that he thought Torrez was a "good hand, working and dependable" but "certain occurances (sic) and acts" of Torrez necessitated "his release from further employment." He considered Torrez "not exactly right mentally and putting it vulgarly speaking I believed he had a loose screw in his head." Hardly enough to convince anybody that Mr. Torrez was insane. On August 4 Judge Jones denied the motion, entered the formal judgment and ordered that Mr. Torrez be executed on October 24. Torrez thanked the judge and told him "I hope when you get there you'll get justice, too."

Now the only thing left to do was to file the notice of appeal, which is almost an automatic act. A form for the notice is in the Penal Code, a secretary types it and the lawyer signs it. It's only one short paragraph and it doesn't have to say why the prisoner is appealing, just that he is appealing; the reasons why are left until the written brief is filed and the case is argued to the Court. But Mr. Hemperley had already taken care of the notice. He filed it as soon as he could after the jury returned with its verdict and sentence on Friday, July 18. He filed it on Monday, the 21st, , the next court day. "Notice is hereby given that the defendant, Simplicio Torrez, hereby appeals from the verdict of conviction rendered in that certain case, wherein the state of Arizona is plaintiff and Simplicio Torrez is defendant, and from the whole thereof. Dated this 21st day of July, A.D. 1919."

That would normally be the end of proceedings in the trial court, but Mr. Hemperley had missed a few things. He appealed "from the verdict of conviction." But in Arizona there is no such thing; an appeal in a criminal case can be only from a formal judgment and when he filed the appeal notice there was no formal judgment; that didn't happen until August 4, seventeen days after the verdict of the jury. And once there was a formal judgment the Arizona Penal Code required a convicted defendant to wait 20 days before he actually filed the notice of appeal (undoubtedly to give the trial court clerk enough time to put the record in shape for the Supreme Court to see). Torrez not only filed his notice before the judgment, but he also did not wait the mandatory 20 days.

As soon as the State learned that, it filed a motion to dismiss the appeal pointing out that the notice was filed too early. It argued that there was no appeal at all because the notice was a nullity and legally the appeal didn't exist.

On December 1, 1919 the Arizona Supreme Court agreed with the state and wrote this opinion:

"PER CURIAM [meaning all of the justices]
On the 4th day of August, 1919, the court rendered judgment and sentenced the appellant to death. On the same day (August 4, 1919) the appellant filed a motion for a new trial, which was overruled. No notice of appeal from the judgment or from the order denying the motion for a new trial was given. In this state of the record we are without jurisdiction to review the case. There is no such thing as an appeal solely from a verdict of guilty, under the provisions of the Penal Code. Penal Code 1913, § 1153. The provisions of the statute, fixing how and when an appeal in a criminal case may be taken to this court, are mandatory and jurisdictional. In Ramon Villalobo v. State, 17 Ariz. 261, 151 Pac. 946, we said: 'the right to appeal is purely a creature of the statute, and where an appeal is not taken within the time prescribed by the law, this court, of course, acquires no jurisdiction, and the judgment of the lower court becomes final and conclusive. This is so well understood by both the bench and bar that it is a waste of words to repeat such a statement of the law. So it may be said in this case that, where an appeal is not taken from a final judgment, or one of the orders mentioned in section 1153, Penal Code, this court, of course, acquires no jurisdiction, and the judgment of the lower court becomes final and conclusive.

It is not a pleasant duty to have to dismiss an appeal without reviewing the case, especially in so grave a case as the present one; but we are powerless and without any discretion in the matter. The appeal is therefore dismissed, with directions to the superior court of Coconino County to proceed with the execution of its judgment."

The Supreme Court Clerk sent a telegram to the Coconino County Attorney: "This is to inform you that the Supreme Court sustained your motion and dismissed the Torez (sic) case with directions to your Superior Court to proceed with execution of its judgment...."

Judge Jones set April 16, 1920 as the new date for execution.

And so it was that Simplicio Torres was hanged by the neck until he was dead on April 16, 1920 at 10 in the morning.

Probably to this day, Simplicio's notice of appeal is still somewhere in the Arizona Supreme Court Clerk's Office with hundreds of other dead and forgotten cases.

I was told that Mr. Hemperley left Flagstaff shortly after that and relocated in California.

The End

Franco's Coat

Even the kitchen was cold that morning. When I left home I put on my raincoat. It wasn't raining but I could just tell from the overcast and the way the wind was blowing through the carport it was going to be nasty and chilly.

I was the first one at the office. I had a preliminary hearing the next day and I wanted to do some work on a few other cases before I went to court. I went to the file room, made a pot of coffee and pulled out some files.

A rape case coming up in a few weeks, a motion in a theft case that would take a day or two next week, a brief on an appeal case ....And then the hearing tomorrow, an insignificant theft case. An old man on Molina Street had been mugged in his house by a couple of kids. They took the old man's money, kicked him in the knees and ran out his back door. He told the police they also took his overcoat but that's not what the kids said after they were caught. Why would they want his clothes, they asked the detective. He was an old man, probably on welfare; they couldn't or wouldn't wear his clothes and they certainly couldn't sell them. Nevertheless, when they were caught one of them had the old man's belt in his pocket.

I took the appeal file and started to look through it to see what research had to be completed before I could start writing. I heard a scratching noise in the lobby. I leaned back in my chair and looked out my office door - nothing, no one had arrived yet and the lights were all off, except for mine. I went back to my work and then I heard a dull knocking. I looked again. Nothing. Then I heard it again. I got up and went into the lobby and turned on the light. Everything was just as it was when I left the night before. Then I glanced at the glass-paneled front door. The tap again. It was an old man in a short-sleeved shirt. He was tapping on the glass. I went to the door and opened it. He came in immediately. He looked cold and he wrapped his arms around his body while he talked very quickly and in a broken accent. As best I could tell, he was Italian.

I gathered he was there because he was to be a witness in a case the office had. I asked the name of the case, but he didn't know. He didn't know the number either, or where or when the case was to be heard. I asked him his name, thinking perhaps I could make a hook-up that way. I didn't understand him. I asked him to spell his name, but he said he couldn't write very well. Then I asked him to say his name again. All I could understand was something like "Franknet." But that didn't sound very Italian - and it didn't mean anything to me. I asked him to say it slowly and I got just about the same thing. I didn't know what else to do so I told him to sit down and that a secretary would be here shortly who could understand him. We didn't have any secretaries who spoke Italian; they spoke Spanish, but maybe that would be close enough. And anyway, better they spend their time with him than me spend my time with him; I was preparing for a number of things and besides....

Then I connected the two – an old Italian man named Franco "Sanetti" ["Franknet"]was the victim in the mugging case I had set for the next day.

I went back to him. He was sitting, staring at the floor with his arms folded and held closely to his sides. I told him who I was, that I was handling the case of State v. Zadillo and that he was the victim in that case. I took his arm and led him into my office. I closed the door and placed him in a chair. I got the file and looked for his written statement. There was a handwritten statement from him but I couldn't read it. I went to the police report and started to read part of it to the old man. When I finished I told him that the hearing was tomorrow and that he could go home because we wouldn't need him until later. He said nothing and I explained to him again – we wouldn't need him until later. He didn't seem to hear me. He just kept saying "my coat" and he made motions like he was putting on an overcoat. I gathered that he was bothered by something about his coat.

"What about your coat?" I asked.

"Boys take," he said.

"You mean the boys who broke into your house took your coat?"

"My coat."

I said that there was no mention in the file about the boys stealing his coat, that the only things they stole were his money and his belt.

"No," he said "my coat…one coat. I'm cold. No coat" and he began to cry.

I felt terrible. Probably the only coat the poor guy had and now those kids had to steal it from him. He obviously couldn't afford another one.

"Why didn't you tell the police that?" I asked.

"I told," he said. Then his voice got louder. "I told them, I told them my coat. The boys take it and run. They should give it back."

"But they said they don't have it," I said. He hung his head and sobbed. "They should give it back."

I didn't know what to do. This old guy was sitting there in his shirt. It was cold on the street and I'll bet he walked all the way here this morning, without a coat or a jacket; he must have been freezing. From the police report I knew about where he lived and I knew it was probably a good bet that he didn't have any heat in his house either. Gees. I really couldn't think of anything reassuring to tell him.

"I'll tell you what I'll do, Mr. Sanetti. I'll call the police. It may be that they do have your coat." Maybe the kids told them where the coat was and maybe the police just forgot to put that down in their report.

He didn't look up.

"It'll take me a little while to do that though. In the meantime I'll have the police take you home. Did you walk down here this morning?"

He didn't react.

"Mr. Sanetti, did you walk here this morning?"

"Yeh," he said.

I got up and took his arm. "Okay, now you sit in the lobby. I'll call the police and have one of them pick you up. We'll do something about your coat. They will take you home and then I'll have them pick you up and bring you back here for the hearing tomorrow. Okay? You just sit down right here and wait."

He slowly lowered himself into the chair. "You get my coat?"

I looked at him trying to show him an expression on my face that said I really did have compassion for him.

"Well, I can't promise you that, Mr.Sanetti, but I'll do the best I can."

I really wasn't sure what that was going to be. I called the police property room and gave them the police report number. I asked the custodian if he would go back to the cubicles and root through the stuff and see if by any chance there was an overcoat there. He asked me if an overcoat was listed in the police report. I said no, but the victim doesn't have one and he says the guys who robbed him also took his coat. He said, "Look, we get a number of people who tell us that the robber took a number of things that were not taken. They're looking for a handout or money from their insurance company. There's not much we can do if it's not listed in the report."

"I know, I know," I told him. "But the old guy says he doesn't have anything. Maybe a mistake was made, maybe there is one, but it just didn't get listed in the report for some reason. Could you please go and look.... Just once.... Thank you."

He said I'd have to hold on while he went down the hall.

I stayed on the line for a few minutes and then he picked up the receiver.

"Well," he said, "I went through everything. There's really nothing there - money, a couple of wallets, cigarettes, a knife, and a belt - all stuff the officers took from the defendants when they arrested them. That's all there is."

"Thank you very much," I said and hung up.

I couldn't imagine the old man had any insurance, but what was I going to tell him. What's he going to do without a coat this winter. Maybe there was some kind of a charity that would give him one.

Then it occurred to me - I had an overcoat I hardly wore. My mom and dad gave it to me when I went away to college in Ohio. Then my wife and I moved to Tucson and the only time I wore it was when we went back east or up into the mountains. But it was old and it had an ugly spot on the right elbow from when I fell on the boardwalk in Atlantic City.

When I went home that night I told my wife.

"What will you do for a coat? she asked.

"Well, I didn't wear one this morning. I took my raincoat; that was enough. That overcoat is too heavy anyway; I always sweated too much when I wore it.

"It's still looks pretty good though," she said.

"Yeh, it does, but you should have seen that old man. He was shivering; he was crying. My God, I felt sorry for him. And those damn kids probably took it as joke - the only one the old guy had. I can get by without one; he can't - for very long at least."

She smiled. "Okay," she said, "let's give him your coat."

I got his address from the police report and drove to his house right after dinner. My wife went with me. She waited in the car as I walked to his door with my coat draped over my arm. I knocked, knocked, and then knocked again. He opened the door and looked at me. He realized who I was and then his eyes went to the coat on my arm.

"Mr. Sanetti ...." I started to say, but he wasn't listening. He put his hands on the coat. His face lit up and he started crying again.

"My coat, my coat."

I tried to explain. "Mr. Sanetti, this isn't...."

He grabbed it and started to put it on. "Yes, my coat."

I guess he didn't notice that it was too big for him.

"Yes, my coat," he said again.

I started to say something, but changed my mind. There wasn't much I could say. It was his coat and now it was returned.

I think he barely noticed when I turned and left.

When I got into the car my wife asked what he said when I handed him the coat.

"He liked it," I said.

The End

A True and Accurate Account of the Execution of Eva Dugan in Arizona in 1930

At 5:01 in the morning, February 21, 1930, Eva Dugan was executed by hanging at the State Prison in Florence, Arizona for the murder of Mr. A.J. Mathis. The execution was dreadful. Some say it caused the Arizona State Legislature to outlaw hanging as a means of execution. Others say it was Ms. Dugan's execution that caused Arizona to repeal capital punishment.

The following is a true and accurate account of her execution and the events that led to it.

Their meeting was accidental – at the Southern Pacific Railroad station where people gathered to greet Santa Claus for his annual appearance in Tucson. It was December 11, 1926. Eva Dugan had just come in from California. She had no job, no place to go, no relatives and little baggage. She was 44, a large woman, robust and experienced. She had been married five times, four ending with her a widow, and one by divorce. Tucson was simply a place to spend some time. Unintentionally, she bumped into A.J. Mathis, a chicken farmer with a ranch four miles outside of Tucson. He was 63 and in good health except for his hearing - he had to use an ear trumpet. He was a quiet man who hoarded things. He lived alone and he was looking for a housekeeper and when he met Ms. Dugan they both decided that she would fill the bill. That afternoon she moved into the Mathis ranch.

About a month later Jack made his appearance. Eva met Jack in Tucson one day as he bummed breakfast from her at the Santa Fe Restaurant. He was a big boy of 19. She brought him home and Mathis hired him as a ranch hand. They called him kid.

On Friday, the 14th of January, Mr. Mathis visited some friends in Tucson and left them late in the afternoon, headed for his ranch in his Dodge coupe. He was never seen again. Eva told everyone she thought he had gone to California to get some money to take care of the mortgage on the ranch. Before he left, she said, he told her to sell his chickens, his cow and his Dodge coupe. On Sunday morning she visited the neighbor closest to the Mathis ranch and told him that Mr. Mathis had gone to Phoenix by train and then was going on to California and would be gone for about a month. When he returned they were going to get married. Oh, and she almost forgot, would he mind looking in on the Mathis ranch for the rest of the day - she and Jack, were going to motor to Nogales for the day. Jack had to go with her, she explained, because she didn't know how to drive. They left that afternoon, Jack was driving.

Two days later they arrived in Lowell, Arizona and they put up at Sander's Auto Camp. Eva registered under the name of B.B. Jones, City, and registered with her was her husband, Jack. The next day Jack and his "wife" left Lowell and a few days later turned up in Amarillo, Texas. There they sold the Dodge coupe executing a bill of sale in the name of A.J. Mathis and received a check for $600 made out to Eva Mathis. From Amarillo they travelled to Kansas City and there they parted company. Jack stayed and Eva went on to White Plains, New York, where she found a job as a nurse. Jack was never seen again.

In Tucson one of Mathis's neighbors became suspicious. Something was amiss. Eva tried to sell her Mathis's cow for $60 and she thought that odd even if Mathis had left for California. His leaving was odd too. He left before; he had relatives in California. But he had never just packed up and gone without saying anything to anyone. And now Eva and Jack disappeared, and with the coupe. They never returned from that day in Nogales. So the neighbor called the Sheriff, James McDonald, and he and his deputies searched the ranch house. In the bottom of the stove they found the charred remains of an ear trumpet and in the barn they found a wrench with blood stains on it. Although the blood stains were believed to be from an animal, they excited everyone's fears and the Sheriff stepped up his investigation. Other neighbors told him that everything had not been rosy between Eva and Mathis. Apparently she tried to poison him, at least that's what Mathis thought. One night right after eating a meal cooked by Eva, Mathis became seriously ill and fired her the next day, telling her to get her things and leave, but she wouldn't and they quarreled. Another neighbor remarked on the frequency of male callers at the ranch when Mr. Mathis went away. And still another neighbor gave the Sheriff a letter he had received from Ceres, California with a signature that appeared to be a very shaky "A.J. Mathis." The relatives in Ceres were contacted and they said that they hadn't heard from him since Christmas. With that, the Sheriff came to the conclusion that A.J. Mathis had been murdered. The towns' people looked for the body but none was found. They searched the ranch, arroyos and the hills for miles around the ranch house but not even a trace of the old man was found.

Eva was easier to trace. Evidence kept turning up from various places about her. The Sheriff tracked her to Texas, to

Chicago, to Buffalo, to New York City, and finally to White Plains, New York where she was working as a nurse under the name of Eva Davis. On February 15, 1927 she was arrested and returned to Tucson to stand trial for stealing Mathis's Dodge coupe. Still there was no trace of A.J. Mathis.

Ms. Dugan said she didn't know where the old man was. As far as she knew he was still in California attending to his mortgage business, and before he left he authorized her to sell his Dodge, and most of the rest of his other property. She admitted she had gone east with Jack and that she wrote the letter from Ceres, California but, she explained, Mr. Mathis asked her to do that. The jury didn't believe her and she was convicted of grand theft. That was in May of 1927 and a few days later she entered the prison at Florence to begin a sentence of three to six years.

Some months later, Mr. J. F. Nash, from Oklahoma, was putting up a tent on the Mathis property not too far from the ranch house. He began to drive a pole into the ground when he noticed that it simply slid in. The ground was soft and mushy. He stood back and noticed that the softness covered a rather large rectangular area and the whole area was depressed and lighter than the surrounding ground. He pulled out the pole and saw a white substance on it. He called one of the neighbors and they agreed it was lime and called the Sheriff.

In the pit was the skeleton of A. J. Mathis; the skull was broken and there was still a gag around its jaw. The body was so badly decomposed that identification had to be made on the basis of the shape of the skull. Mr. Mathis's barber, who had been cutting the old man's hair for years, and others who knew the old man, said it looked like the skull of A. J. Mathis.

Shortly before Christmas 1927 Eva Dugan was charged with the willful and premeditated murder of A. J. Mathis and a trial date was set. Until then she had said nothing about the case. The case against her was purely circumstantial and the prosecution expected no help from her. They and the town knew her story and it didn't involve the killing of A. J. Mathis. But they were all in for a surprise.

When Eva Dugan took the stand in her own defense she said the testimony she gave at her grand theft trial was a lie and she was present when A. J. Mathis died. "But it wasn't murder," she said, "it was more like a terrible accident."

She said Jack did it but it wasn't really meant to be what it looked like. After supper on the evening she and Jack were to leave

66

for Nogales, Mr. Mathis and Jack went to catch some chickens to sell the following morning. Soon after they left she saw Jack running away but he got caught in a barbed wire fence. She went to him and asked what happened. He told her that Mr. Mathis wanted him to milk the cow. When he told the old man that he couldn't, Mr. Mathis "popped him upon the side of the head there" (she pointed to the right side of her head), then continued, "and he said, 'what in the hell are you good for,' slapped him, and the kid just throwed his arm around there like that, carelessly - didn't think it was such a blow, caught him right there and he fell backwards. He was weak and sick in the stomach here anyway, and just a blow like that, unexpected to him, would knock him over, knock him down and he fell. What wind was left in him I guess went out when he fell. It was hard there. There was nothing at all, but just pure hard ground." She and Jack tried to revive him but they couldn't. So, Jack took him away and didn't come back until much later that night. She never asked what Jack had done with the body and she didn't want to know, she said. They decided it wouldn't look good if they told everybody exactly what happened so they then decided to tell a story about Mr. Mathis having to go to California and asking Eva to sell his property. After planting their story with the neighbors, they left for Dalhart, Texas for a "good time."

The trial lasted a week. The jury went out at six o'clock on a Friday night and came back with a verdict in less than three hours – guilty with a penalty of death.

Eva made no outcry or showed any emotion as the verdict was read. She just leaned forward in her chair and stared. The judge set the execution for March 6, 1928 and when it was over she turned to Sheriff McDonald and said, "Well, I guess you're satisfied now," and stalked off to her cell surrounded by guards.

March 6 was not as close as it appeared. It would come and go twice before it was all over. Ms. Dugan appealed her case to the Arizona Supreme Court. When they denied her appeal she applied to the Board of Pardons and Paroles for a commutation and that too was denied. Her last effort was to have herself declared insane, which under state law would make her unsuitable for execution. But that didn't work either when a jury in Pinal County found that she was mentally fit and ready for hanging. The date for execution was reset to February 21, 1930.

Letters started to come in to state newspapers deploring the fact that there was such a thing as the death penalty and praying that it not be used against a woman, especially a woman like Eva who was convicted only on circumstantial evidence. One letter said: "No circumstantial evidence should be taken as absolute when a human life is at stake. I am not contending that this woman is innocent, but I believe it is essential to the safety of all innocent people that the death penalty should not be imposed on circumstantial evidence, even if it seems much stronger than it does in this case..."

The Disabled Veterans sent a lengthy petition to the Governor pleading for clemency. The Governor said "My hands are tied....Even though I wanted to do something I could not. The law does not empower me to grant a reprieve or commutation."

A defense fund was started to save Ms. Dugan. "We have only eight days and will have to work fast," was a quote from one of the founders, Mrs. John H. Durham. "I have seen two innocent men hanged on circumstantial evidence, and I do not believe that Mrs. Dugan has received justice. I believe that the sentence should be commuted or stayed until Jack, the boy who has been implicated in the case, can be found."

The American League to Abolish Capital Punishment, Inc. of New York City joined the fight by sending Mrs. Ruth Hale to Tucson to confer with officials. Mrs. Hale, in addition to her duties with the League, was also president of the Lucy Stone League which advocated the retention of maiden names by married women. "It is a horrible thing," she told newsmen upon her arrival, "to take a human being, and, with measured step lead him or her to the shambles, as one might do an ox or a lamb. Whenever a prisoner is thus cold-bloodedly done to death by the law something happens inside of the inmates. Something is turned over inside of them." And with this, went the newspaper article, "she tightened her lips and twisted her small clenched white hand in an expressive gesture."

$64 was collected for the defense fund and a death watch was placed over Ms. Dugan by the prison. Her execution would take place as scheduled.

Contrary to normal prison practice, Ms. Dugan was given permission to be executed in the white silk shroud she made for herself in prison just for the execution. Since her stay in prison she made handkerchiefs and beadwork and sold them to fellow prisoners and visitors. With that money and a small amount she collected from newsmen once she knew that she was going to die, Ms. Dugan bought her own coffin and hired a private undertaker to prepare her body for burial. She was also given permission to have two lady friends with her the night before the execution. They sat and played whist and drank lemonade. Then at one o'clock in the morning of her last day, Ms. Dugan was removed from her cell and put into a cell in a different building. One of her whist partners had informed the warden that Ms. Dugan inquired what she would do if it were her – "wait for the noose or cheat it." Eva told the partner that she had hidden away a bottle of poison and some razor blades. After she was taken from her cell, a search was made and a small bottle of ammonia was discovered under her mattress, with some razor blades.

Shortly before four in the morning Ms. Dugan was readied for execution. It was overcast and a light rain fell as two guards escorted her from her temporary cell to the building that housed the hanging apparatus. Over 70 people were squeezed into a small room to observe. Most were newsmen who were there to cover the first execution of a woman in Arizona and the 23rd execution in Arizona's history. Other witnesses were exactly that, witnesses required by law to attend an execution. Six of the spectators were women, two from Tucson, all six part of a protest against the barbarity of capital punishment.

When she reached the platform a guard put the hemp noose around her neck and the warden asked her if she wanted to say anything. She paused, looked about and then said something only the warden and the hangman could hear. A black cap was placed over her head, the noose tightened and the signal given to release the trap. What happened was horrible.

When the trap was released the body of Ms. Dugan dropped through the opening and crumpled on the floor below, headless. The force of the jolt had snapped the vertebrae, "already wasted from a long-standing social disease," the newspapers said, and the head was flung to the floor several feet from the body. Spectators could see the chin and mouth of Ms. Dugan under the black cap.

The prison chaplain, who was a staunch foe of capital punishment, and a spectator shouted, "You who believe in capital punishment take a look, women first."

When it was over, the prison officials were interviewed. They described Ms. Dugan's attitude as "one of resignation and gratitude for what had been done in her behalf," and her approach to the execution as "graceful." Then the warden was asked to repeat what she said to him at the last moment when she was on the scaffolding waiting for the noose to be tightened. He said he asked her if she had anything to say and she replied "I have nothing to say, bless them all, the filthy bastards."

And so ends the true and accurate account of the trials and subsequent justifiable homicide of Eva Dugan in Tucson in 1930.

Postscript

Hanging as a means of execution was not abolished until four years after her execution. Arizona repealed its death penalty once, but that was 14 years before the murder of Mr. Mathis and it was restored two years later. In early statehood hanging was the official means of execution. Execution is now by lethal injection.

The End

The Most Dangerous Rat

On May 10, 1933 Indiana Governor Paul V. McNutt opened an era of violence when he signed the parole papers for prisoner #13225 at the Indiana State Prison and twelve days later prisoner #13225 walked out of the prison a free man. Never again, except for one short interval, would he be held in any jail anywhere. His freedom ended in June of the following year - just 13 months but to some it seemed like an eternity. Prisoner #13225 was John Dillinger.

Once out of prison, John Dillinger lost no time picking up where he left off as a juvenile delinquent. In his first month of freedom he and two cohorts committed four robberies and an aggravated assault. Two weeks later, after shooting his first man in an attempt to rob a mill in Monticello, Indiana, he joined up with veteran bank robbers, Harry "Pete" Pierpont and James "Bobbie" Clark. By Christmas, 1933, the three had committed five robberies, killed three people and stole $150,000 in cash. The newspapers followed him closely and were entertained by his flamboyant behavior. He was dapper, well dressed, mannerly, and on more than one occasion vaulted over the bank's counter to get the money.

In January 1934, with a number of warrants outstanding for their arrest he and his gang decided they were due for a rest and they headed for Tucson, Arizona.

The story there begins on a drizzly, gloomy Monday morning, January 22. A brand new Studebaker made its way along the only route into town from the north and stopped at the Tucson Realty & Trust Company. Two men and a woman said they were looking for a house to rent for a month or two while vacationing in the city. Charles Clapp, the young man tending the office that morning, told them about the home of Mrs. Hattie Strauss at 927 N. 2nd Street. Her husband worked for the Southern Pacific Railroad, he told them, and about this time each year he made an extended trip to Mexico, 65 miles to the south. When her husband did this, the young realtor explained, Mrs. Strauss stayed in an apartment and rented the house to winter visitors.

The oldest of the three visitors was Charles Makley, a recent addition to the Dillinger clan, wanted on warrants from three states for murder, bank robbery and assault. The other two were Bobbie Clark and his girlfriend, Opal "Mack Truck" Long. Clark was wanted by two states for murder and bank robbery. Mrs. Strauss was asking $200 a month and $25 in escrow for breakage of her China. Makley, posing as Mr. Davies, took $15 from a thick roll of bills and put it into her hand. He would guarantee, he said, that nothing would be broken. Because of the condition of the house the newcomers couldn't move in for a few days but they all agreed that was all right; they would stay some place temporarily and then come back. Mrs. Strauss suggested the Congress Hotel.

The next day the Congress Hotel caught fire and in the midst of it, Firemen William Benedict and Kenneth Pender put up a ladder to the second floor and evacuated a number of guests. Among the people they evacuated were Clark, Makley and Long. The three seemed overly concerned about saving their clothes and personal belongings, the firemen remembered. And when they reached the ground Makley refused to go across the street to a safety zone. He insisted the firemen put the ladder back up and retrieve the belongings from their rooms. "I have several valuables I want to get," he said, pointing toward the third floor. But the ladder, the firemen told him, only went to the second floor and because of the intensity of the flames they did not feel that a few personal belongings were worth the risk. Clark, who was in his pajamas, suggested that if the firemen put the ladder up to the second floor he and his friend would walk up to the third floor and retrieve the possessions. The firemen agreed and Makley and Clark scrambled up the ladder, through the second floor, up a flight of stairs and then soon reappeared at a window holding pieces of luggage and a very large and heavy trunk. Benedict helped the two carry the luggage to the street while Pender struggled with the trunk; Clark wouldn't let him throw it or slide it down the ladder; he wanted it carried. When they got everything across the street and into the drug store where the fleeing guests were gathered, Clark offered the firemen a tip. They refused but when Clark insisted, they each took $6.

The older, portly man (Makley), looked familiar to fireman Benedict and when the fire was controlled and Benedict had some time to himself at the station, he leafed through a "True" magazine he read just a few days before. The face of the portly man with the heavy trunk seemed to match a picture in the magazine. The picture was of Charles Makley, bespectacled member of the infamous Dillinger gang. Benedict and Pender mentioned this to a friend at the Pima County Sheriff's Office and they told him about the heavy trunk, but nothing happened.

January 24, windy, clear – ropes surrounded what was left of the Congress Hotel and debris was removed and sifted all day long.

That morning two more brand new cars arrived in Tucson. In a Buick were Harry Pierpont and his girlfriend, Mary Kinder. They came west, they later told newsmen, to get away from the bad weather in the east. As soon as they arrived they went to a small auto court on South 6th Street, unpacked and then began looking for a home to rent for a month or so. They put $130 down on one and returned to the auto court. The second car was a Hudson; it belonged to John Dillinger and his companion, Billie Fretchett. They also registered at an auto court on South 6th Street and went looking for a home to rent.

Later that day, Pierpont and Mary Kinder ran a stop sign close to South 6th Street and as they did they noticed they were being watched by a police car and two patrolmen. The policemen were Earl Nolan and "Swede" Walker, both traffic officers. Nolan stopped the car and as he approached the Buick he noticed it had Florida license plates. He decided not to issue a ticket but he cautioned the driver to be more careful, especially with such a new car and the driver gave him a tip. As he talked to them he saw what struck him as smart luggage in the rear seat.

Thursday, January 25, clear and bright. That morning a "smoking hot tip" came in to the police station and was immediately passed along to the Chief, C. A. Wollard - who was eating lunch at home –the Dillinger gang was in town and they were staying at Mrs. Strauss's house. Within minutes, Wollard got a squad of his best men together at the station. He told them what had happened and told them to be cautious.

He directed four men to the Strauss house and as they approached the house, they noticed a late model Studebaker with Florida license plates in the driveway but no other cars. The window shades were drawn and the house seemed quiet. They decided they would surround the house and set up surveillance but as they were positioning themselves they noticed a middle aged man come out the front door with a young woman. He appeared to be a businessman about to leave for work – glasses, dark hair, about 45 or 50, with a chubby face and he walked with a limp. When they got into the Studebaker and drove away, the police followed. They were Charles Makley and his girlfriend. Makley was arrested at Grabes Electric Retail Store as he was attempting to purchase a short wave radio and at the station he gave his name as

J.L. Davies, a winter visitor from Florida. The girl refused to give her name. When the police examined the Studebaker they found nothing, except for one thing that struck Officer Nolan – luggage, the same type he had seen in a car the night before and he remembered that that car was also from Florida. On their way to the police station, Makley asked the officers to please take him by his house so that he might provide them with more complete identification. They refused and when they got to the station they compared his face and fingerprints with a bulletin from the "American Bankers Protection Association." J.L. Davies was Charles Makley, a member of the Dillinger gang. Now the newspapers were notified.

Back at the Strauss' house, officers prepared to surround it and use a trick to gain entrance. Chet Sherman went to the front door, a paper in his hand, as if he were delivering something and Eyman and Mullaney went to the rear door. Dallas Ford stayed close behind Sherman and out of sight. Sherman knocked on the door and a woman appeared. That was "Mack Truck" Opal Long. She took the letter and was just about to close the door when Sherman pushed it open and rushed in. James Clark, who was in his shorts, jumped up, grabbed Sherman and threw him to the floor. Sherman tried to draw his gun but he couldn't get to it. Ford heard the scuffle and rushed to the door when Mack Truck closed it on his hand, breaking a finger. When he eventually got the front door open he jumped on Clark just as Eyman and Mullaney broke in the back door.

Along with Clark and Mack Truck the officers confiscated two Thompson sub-machineguns, one 45 caliber machinegun, one tank gun (chambered for super-powerful .351 caliber rifle bullets), two steel and velvet bullet-proof vests, two hand guns, hundreds of rounds of ammunition, a sawed-off shotgun and two pistols. At the police station Clark identified himself as Art Taylor, a businessman. Opal Long gave her correct name and nothing more.

Within minutes after the capture of Clark and Long, another car, a new Buick with Florida tags, pulled up to the Strauss home. A man and woman got out and walked toward the front door. The man was tall, thin, dark, with a sloping, thin face and a blunt, hawk nose. He was fairly well dressed. The woman seemed impatient. They rang the doorbell but no one answered and the man went around to the back door. When he returned, he shook his head no, and then both started toward the Buick. Halfway down the sidewalk they stopped and stared at something on the walk. The man leaned down, wiped his finger in the "something" and then put it to his nose. They both said something then hurriedly got into the car and drove away.

Just about this time patrolmen Nolan and Eyman were sent to cruise South 6th Street to look for the Buick Nolan had seen the day before with the spiffy-looking luggage. They spotted the car going south out of town, toward Mexico, a man driving and a young woman at his side. The back was stuffed with luggage – just like Makley's. Eyman signaled the car over to the side of the road and told Nolan to stay back and keep an eye on the driver. Then he approached the Buick. He told the driver he noticed that he was from out of state and that in Arizona a car must have an inspection sticker before it can be used on the state highways. Very politely, the driver told him that he was from Florida and was unfamiliar with the ways of Arizona. Eyman informed him that since he was from Florida and not a fulltime resident he should get a special sticker to protect him while he was vacationing in Tucson, but he would have to get it at the police station. Eyman even suggested that he would ride with them to guide them to the station. The driver agreed and Eyman got into the back seat, which was so full of luggage he had to sit on top of the bags. On the way, they small-talked and Eyman sat with his hand on his concealed gun. Pierpont later told newsmen that he too had a gun drawn and on the seat next to him.

When they arrived at the city hall they went directly to the Chief's office. Eyman held the door open for the girl to enter first, then Pierpont, and as he entered he saw the luggage seized from Clark and Makley, and machine gun boxes piled on the floor.

Pierpont started to draw a gun from his vest pocket but Eyman drew first. Pierpont stopped, smiled and then began to reach into another pocket. Eyman jammed his gun into Pierpont's side. His glasses fell off his nose and he dropped his hands to his sides. "You're treatin' me pretty rough, aren't you?' Pierpont said. When Eyman relaxed, Pierpont stuffed a small piece of paper into his mouth and Eyman grabbed him by the neck. "Spit it out," he yelled. "Spit it out." Pierpont wrestled with him and Chief Wollard got a pair of "come alongs" and slapped them onto Pierpont's arms. Then Eyman forced his mouth open. The piece of paper had an address on it – 1304 East Fifth. Eyman knew the home; it was owned by a winter visitor from Minnesota – a home that he usually rented out for a good part of the winter. Pierpont gave his name as

J.C. Evans; business, tourist. His girlfriend gave her correct name, Mary Kinder.

While Pierpont and his girlfriend were being booked, Officers Walker, Mullaney and Herron were sent to watch 927 North Second and Eyman and Nolan went to 1304 East Fifth.

Walker waited inside the house on Second Street, Herron outside, across the street and out of sight, and Mullaney was up the street with the car. In a few minutes a new Hudson pulled up a short distance from the front door. A slim, good looking man wearing glasses got out, looked about and then made his way toward the house. Behind him sitting in the car was a young woman. Just as he reached the front door, Walker opened it and pointed a shotgun at him. At the same time Herron came out of his hiding place across the street with his gun drawn. Mullaney covered the Hudson and ordered the woman to get out and put her hands on the roof. Although they had no idea who the man and woman were, they decided to arrest them. Walker confronted the good looking man with the glasses. "Wait there," he said, "we're going to arrest you." The man smiled and pressed one arm tightly against his side. Walker took a step toward him and lowered the shotgun. "I said we're going to arrest you – don't go for nothin'." Then Walker told Herron to search him. Herron told the man to get his hands up and then he moved quickly about the man, feeling his coat, his pants and his vest. He didn't have any weapons. The woman had a smart, snappy set of luggage.

The man said his name was John Sullivan; the woman gave her name as Ann Martin. He told the police that they were married but the woman denied it. They were booked and the man's fingerprints were compared against the fingerprints from the banking association bulletin. It was John Dillinger. $8850 in cash was removed from his suitcase - $6500 in a flour sack, $350 in new five dollar bills and some $2000 from a money belt.

And that was it; it was over. In one day the John Dillinger gang was captured and not a shot was fired.

Immediately, five states wanted the fugitives. All wired Tucson that their agents were on the way to claim them. Five days later Dillinger was put on a plane to Crown Point, Indiana where he was to stand trial for the murder of a deputy sheriff during a bank robbery, but John Dillinger was never tried. Two weeks after he was returned to Crown Point, he escaped – this time for good.

"He just walked out," said the prosecutor. He used a wooden pistol and fooled everyone. "If I ever see John Dillinger," said the woman sheriff, "I'll shoot him through the head with my own pistol." She never did and Dillinger wasn't seen again until July 23, 1934. This time, the last time, in Chicago, Illinois.

Melvin H. Purvis, the head Chicago agent for the F.B.I., had received information earlier that day that Dillinger was going to attend the evening performance of "Manhattan Melodrama," a movie starring Clark Gable and William Powell, at the Biograph theater.

Purvis and twelve men covered the theater that night. Every door was checked and watched and soon Dillinger appeared. The agents watched him buy a ticket and then sat back and waited while he watched the movie. Purvis was in his car, a slight distance away when Dillinger appeared with two women. "He was coatless," said Purvis, "but wore a hat and gold rimmed spectacles."

When Dillinger left the show Purvis alerted his men and Dillinger attempted to run away but as soon as he pulled his gun he was hit with a number of shots and killed. His body was taken to the Alexian Brothers Hospital, but it wouldn't admit him because he was dead. So the body was laid on the grass in front of the hospital with a police guard nearby.

Purvis refused to give out the names of the men who had fired on Dillinger. "There were two or three men who fired," he said. "I was not one of them, but they were federal agents."

While Dillinger's body lay outside the hospital people gathered and took souvenirs – pieces of paper and handkerchiefs dipped in Dillinger's blood, the bricks where he fell, and even the shirt he was wearing.

In Tucson, Police Chief Wollard said, "The country is better off without him." J. Edgar Hoover told the reporters that Dillinger "didn't say a word before he died…We didn't give him a chance. He was the most dangerous rat this country has ever known."

The End

Rules of Court

Rules of Deportment for Division 218 of the Superior Court

Perhaps a few words are in order about rules. First, let me say that I agree with Wordsworth – "A few strong instincts, and a few plain rules." Now, some instincts:

As he (Einstein) was a late talker, his parents were worried. At last, at the supper table one night, he broke his silence *to say, "The soup is too hot." Greatly relieved, his parents asked why he had never said a word before. Albert replied, "Because up to now everything was in order."*

It seems to me that if everything is in order by the time you get to court (and it probably will be) you don't have to say much. So –

RULE 1

Say only what is necessary. Often, the Court will be able to grasp your argument the first time you state it. So in most cases it isn't necessary to repeat it. Also keep in mind that the Court's vocabulary is rather limited. It knows and can use some words, but not many.

Try to use familiar words that everyone will understand. Churchill agreed. He said: *Short words are best and the old words when short are best of all.*

RULE 2.

Don't feel obligated to take all the time the minute entry gives you. If the minute entry gives you 15 minutes and you need only 5, hooray, don't take any more. Everyone will appreciate it.

And I like arguments that come alive with graphics - charts, handouts, photos, slides, movies, whatever. I hear it a lot better when I can see it. Whenever I see that picture of Clark Gable about to carry Vivien Leigh up that majestic stairway in Tara, it comes alive when I hear him say*: You've turned me out while you chased Ashley Wilkes, while you dreamed of Ashley Wilkes. This is one night you're not turning me out.*

RULE 3.

The time for oral argument will be limited and stated in the minute entry setting the hearing (except for opening and closing arguments at trial - but even then I will probably set some limits occasionally). Each side in a case will have 15 minutes to argue a motion for summary judgment. If there are two parties on a side they will split the 15 minutes - and that includes rebuttal.

If you need more time (you should realize even in the U.S. Supreme Court you get but 30 minutes) ask for it by motion. My inclination is to not give more, but it could happen.

RULE 4.

Please stick to the Rules of Civil Procedure and all the other rules in the Arizona Revised Statutes. I am aware that Leo Durocher said *I believe in rules? Sure I do. If there weren't any rules, how could you break them?* But he played games (baseball). We don't. It sure will make things easier if we all follow the rules.

RULE 5.

Rarely will I ask you to go beyond the page limits in the Rules. If I want you to I will say so in a minute entry. If you feel a larger calling requires you to go beyond the limit please let me know beforehand, by motion, what that *"calling"* is and why it thinks you should have more.

RULE 6

Dress is not optional; everyone must be dressed to get in the courtroom, but garment variations are tolerated - to a degree. I think all males should wear suits or sport jackets, ties, long pants, and non-sneakers. If you forget to bring a tie I can loan you one - but I want it back (for the next guy).

Consider the story about Mark Twain. *He was careless about his dress. One day he called on Harriet Beecher Stowe without his necktie. On his return Mrs. Clemens noticed the omission and scolded him. A little later a messenger turned up on Ms. Stowe's doorstep and handed her a small package. Inside was a black necktie, and a note: "Here is a necktie. Take it out and look at it. I think I stayed half an hour this morning without this necktie. At the end of that time, will you kindly return it, as it is the only one I have. Mark Twain."*

I can't supply you with any other apparel so you may want to have a court "suit" handy at the office, just in case you forgot to make a note of your courtroom appearance.

Another interesting anecdote in this regard is told about

Guines (Adrien-Louis de Bonnieres, Duke of Guines), French diplomat and ambassador to London in the late 1770's. *He was enormously fat, but nonetheless a great dandy. His wardrobe contained two pairs of breeches for each outfit - one for days when he would have to sit down and the other, much tighter, for days when he would only have to stand. In the morning his valet's first question would be: "Will monsieur be sitting down today?"*

Like the Duke, you must have your attire at ready because you just may be sitting down today.

Women should wear something "appropriate." Having never dressed as a woman does, I take that to mean something you would wear to a meeting at which you want to impress someone.

And both sexes should keep this in mind: *There is one other reason for dressing well, namely that dogs respect it, and will not attack you in good clothes. (Ralph Waldo Emerson)*

RULE 7.

Court starts on time, 9 in the morning, 1:30 in the afternoon. We end at noon and 4:45 and take two 15 minute breaks, one in the morning, one in the afternoon. It's possible that if you're not there at starting time court will begin anyway.

Another cogent anecdote: *Edward Marsh was waiting at a railroad station with Mrs. Churchill for Churchill to join them to catch a train. It was getting late and Mrs. Churchill began to worry that her husband would miss the train. Marsh soothed her by observing, "Winston is such a sportsman that he always gives the train a chance to get away."*

Don't give my bailiff the opportunity; we just may get away without you.

RULE 8.

Formality in the courtroom will be kept to a minimum. I do realize I am the judge, I wear a robe, and I sit higher than everybody else, but "M'lord" is unnecessary.

"Bill" is really too informal, but "Judge" or "Your Honor" will do.

RULE 9.

I eat lunch, almost always, in my office. But I lock the door. I've found that if I don't, all sorts of people will want access to me. Also, I am in my chambers between 7:30 and 8 in the morning, but I try not to see people (lawyers, citizens, whoever) until 8:45. If you have something you think I just gotta see during those "interlude" times, slip it under the door.

I also have a nifty ruse for cutting short an all-too-long conference. I got it from Bismarck. *He had been conversing for rather a long time with the English ambassador when the latter posed the question "How do you handle insistent visitors who take up so much of our valuable time?" Bismarck answered, "Oh, I have an infallible method. My servant appears and informs me that my wife has something urgent to tell me." At that moment there was a knock at the door and the servant entered with a message from his wife.*

Not bad - sort of like "I'll have to hang up now; I've got a call I've been waiting for."

RULE 10.

By the time you get to court I will have read what you filed. That means if you see your way clear, you only have to talk about those things you didn't put in your pleadings. I don't see much use in telling me what I've already read.

RULE 11.

Not all "oral argument requested" will get argument. Some just don't seem to need it. If the purpose of argument is to help me make a decision, I don't need it in some cases - I don't need anything more than the pleadings in some cases.

RULE 12.

I don't have re-cross examination; you'll get all the time you need on cross examination, but then it's over - the fat lady will have sung. What that means is that you'd better get all your good stuff in the first time around. And it won't help that the other guy brought up something "new" on redirect - you should have objected to that.

RULE 13.

I hold court on Monday, Tuesday, Wednesday, Thursday, and Friday. Sorry.

RULE 14.

I hold cases on the inactive calendar for 90 days. I do that so I don't lose track of them. I have trouble remembering things that are older than 90 days - after all, the Spanish-American war didn't last that long and I hardly remember that at all.

* * * * * * *

"Proceed. You have my biased attention."
(Learned Hand to a lawyer asking for reconsideration of a ruling)

The italicized anecdotes; Einstein and those in Rules 6, 7, and 9, are taken from *"The Little, Brown Book of Anecdotes,"* edited by Clifton Fadiman.

Clark Gable's quote is taken from *The Dictionary of Film Quotations* by Melinda Corey and George Ochoa.

Churchill's quote can be found in *Familiar Quotations* by John Bartlett.

Emerson's quote is from http://www.goodreads.com;

Durocher's quote is from *Nice Guys Finish Last* by Leo Durocher with Ed Linn, University of Chicago Press.

Judge Hand's quote is "unsourced." I found its latest iteration in Wikiquote.org/wiki/LearnedHand.

You might also enjoy the colloquy between the judge and a juror in *United States v. Thompson*, 744 F.2d 1065 (4th Cir.1984).

The End

Sources and Attributions

Schmid: "The Pied Piper of Tucson" by Don Moser and Jerry Cohen; "The Tucson Murders" by John Gilmore; The Tucson Star and The Tucson Citizen newspapers; the Arizona Republic newspaper; Preliminary Hearing and Trial transcripts; Arizona State Supreme Court Reports.

Old Drum: Missouri Historical Society; Classics of The Bar, by Alvin V. Sellers ,Vol. 2 "Senator Vest's Tribute To The Dog."

Simplicio Torrez: The Coconino Sun newspaper; The Arizona Republic newspaper.

Eva Dugan: Arizona State Prison Records, The Arizona Republic newspaper. Arizona State Historical Society Records.

Dillinger: The Tucson Star and The Tucson Citizen newspapers; The Dillinger Days by John Tolan; John Dillinger, The Life and Death of America's First Celebrity Criminal by Dary Matera.